WINGS AT THE READY

Seventy-Fifth Anniversary
Naval Air Reserve
1916-1991

WINGS AT

THE READY

75 Years of the Naval Air Reserve

Editor in Chief: Captain Anthony Turpin, USNR

Author: Commander Richard Shipman, USNR

Photo Director: Commander Peter Mersky, USNR

Chief Photographer: Mr. George Hall

Naval Institute Press

Annapolis, Maryland

This book would not have been possible without the generous support of the following companies:

BEECHCRAFT CORPORATION
SERV-AIR INCORPORATED
LOCKHEED CORPORATION
GRUMMAN CORPORATION
SIKORSKY AIRCRAFT
McDONNELL DOUGLAS AIRCRAFT
LITTON SYSTEMS INCORPORATED
KAY & ASSOCIATES
GULFSTREAM CORPORATION

Library of Congress Cataloging-in-Publication Data

Shipman, Richard, 1944–
    Wings at the ready: 75 years of the Naval Air Reserve / editor in chief, Anthony Turpin; author, Richard Shipman; photo director, Peter Mersky; chief photographer, George Hall.
        p.   cm.
    ISBN 1-55750-750-3
    1. United States.   Naval Air Reserve—History.   I. Turpin, Anthony.   II. Title.
VG94.7.S55   1991
359.9′43—dc20   91-20039
                                                                          CIP

Printed in the United States of America on acid-free paper ∞
9 8 7 6 5 4 3 2
First printing

Front Endpaper: Various Lockheed aircraft used by the Naval Air Reserve: (*back row*) T-1A Seastar, P-2 Neptune, PV-2 Harpoon, and (*front row*) C-130 Hercules, P-3 Orion, and S-3 Viking. (Painting by Captain Ted Wilbur, courtesy Lockheed Aeronautical Systems Corporation)

Back Endpaper: Naval Air Reserve FA-18 and F-14 (Painting by Captain Ted Wilbur, American Society of Aviation Artists)

CONTENTS

Greetings from President George Bush vii

Flag Officers' Salutations ix

Preface by Admiral Chambers, Commander, Naval Air Reserve xi

Acknowledgments xiii

Glossary of Abbreviations and Acronyms xv

1. The Naval Air Reserve Today 1

2. The Naval Air Reserve Is Born 15

3. A New Era for the Naval Air Reserve 38

4. The *Pueblo* Call-up: Success from Adversity 55

5. Reorganization 62

6. Horizontal Integration: Equality for the Reserve 82

7. Reinforcing and Sustaining Units 96

8. Naval Air Reserve Bases and Stations 107

9. The Next 75 Years 160

    Appendix A. Shapers of the Naval Air Reserve 169

    Appendix B. Major Commands of the Naval Air Reserve 173

    Appendix C. Aircraft and Squadrons of the Naval Air Reserve 181

THE WHITE HOUSE

WASHINGTON

December 18, 1990

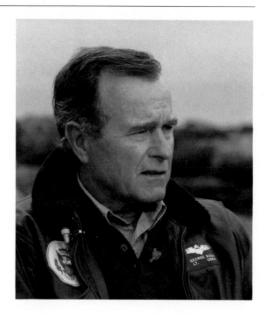

I am pleased to extend my warmest greetings and congratulations to everyone celebrating the 75th anniversary of the Naval Air Reserve.

Naval Reserve aviators have written a proud chapter in the annals of our Nation's Armed Forces—a chapter filled with accounts of the courage and dedication demonstrated by America's citizen-sailors. From their participation in World War II to the present deployment in the Persian Gulf, and on countless other occasions, the members of the Naval Air Reserve have earned a reputation for bravery and professionalism in defending the principles that we hold dear.

As a ready supply of talent, the Reserves have long been valued as a vital component of our Armed Forces, and they have contributed immeasurably to the defense of our Nation. In keeping with this honorable tradition, Naval Reserve Aviation continues to help keep our Sea Services ready to defend peace and freedom around the world; and it gives me great pleasure to salute your members, past and present, for your devoted service to America.

Barbara joins me in sending our best wishes for your next 75 years of service. God bless you.

George Bush

FLAG OFFICER SALUTATIONS

ACNO, Air Warfare, Vice Admiral R. M. Dunleavy

The Naval Air Reserve has, over the years, consistently provided significant and cost-effective contributions helping the Navy meet its worldwide commitments . . . a constant in the ever-changing environment of world events the Naval Air Reserve is at the leading edge of the Navy's efforts to fully integrate active and reserve components . . . the well earned, rich heritage of the Naval Air Reserve is sincerely appreciated, Keep Strokin. . . .

R. M. DUNLEAVY
Vice Admiral, U.S. Navy

Chief of Naval Reserve, Rear Admiral J. E. Taylor

Over the past 75 years Naval Aviation and the Naval Air Reserve have evolved into a superb, complementary Total Force. This evolution can be traced through every major conflict—and many minor ones—in this country.

But the real heroes of this remarkable story are the men and women of the Naval Air Reserve Force—the leaders who have worked so tirelessly to acquire fleet-compatible aircraft and equipment for training: the dedicated pilots, NFOs, air crewmen, maintenance and ground support personnel; and all the talented Naval Reservists who keep our aircraft in the air, ready to provide mutual support or to mobilize in defense of our country.

It is these outstanding men and women that this volume really honors. This is their story, and I salute them.

J. E. TAYLOR
Rear Admiral, U.S. Navy

Dedication

In the famous conclusion to James Michener's book *The Bridges of Toko-Ri*, the crusty admiral stands on the bridge of his aircraft carrier and muses about the recent death of one of his pilots in combat over Korea. "Why is America lucky enough to have such men? They leave this tiny ship and fly against the enemy. They then must seek the ship, lost somewhere on the sea. And when they find it, they have to land upon its pitching deck. Where did we get such men?"

The pilot whose death prompted these immortal words was Lieutenant Harry Brubaker, United States Naval Reserve. Like thousands of citizen-soldiers before and after him, he had been called from his civilian life to help support the goals of the United States. Leaving his law firm and family behind while he flew from pitching decks over the hostile terrain of Korea was no easier for Brubaker than other mobilizations have been for the thousands of reservists who have been called by their country. But they have responded, and responded well, to crises ranging from localized hostilities to world wars.

The Naval Air Reserve has many reasons to celebrate on its 75th anniversary. Never has it been better equipped. Never have its people been better trained or more capable. Never has it been more able to accomplish its mission. For the first time in its history, the Naval Air Reserve is flying state-of-the-art aircraft such as F/A-18s, F-14s, and P-3s alongside their active-duty counterparts. Reserve squadrons enjoy sufficient funding to support pilots' readiness and maintain their aircraft. Yet even with the great strides made in hardware, funding, and support, the secret to the Naval Air Reserve's success has been and always will be the motivation and dedication of its people. This book is dedicated to those people.

PREFACE

The statues of Revolutionary War volunteers—the minutemen who played such an important role in our nation's struggle for independence—which stand in cities and towns across the country, serve as a lasting tribute to the "citizen soldiers" who answered the very first American call to arms. In that war, Americans dropped their plows and left farms and shops to pick up musket and shot and do battle in the name of freedom. When it was over and they had won, the "minutemen" put away their arms and returned to their fields, their homes and shops . . . until called again. And they were indeed, called again, and again! The challenge of every conflict, every war, has been met head-on by citizens who hear and responded to the call.

From the notion that we should have a volunteer military whose members are its nation's citizens, has evolved a need for a well-equipped, well-trained reserve, to augment our active forces.

The Naval Air Reserve is a strategic component of that force. What began 75 years ago as a flying militia with a handful of pilots has, over the decades, been shaped by men of vision and the circumstance of war. In World Wars One and Two, Korea, in many emergencies, and most recently in the Persian Gulf, men and women of the Naval Air Reserve stood proudly alongside their active-duty counterparts in service to our country. F. Trubee Davison, David Ingalls, Jack Shea, George Bush, and thousands of others have built the Naval Air Reserve on a tradition of excellence, patriotism, and dedication. It is to them that this book is dedicated and to the "minutemen and women" who are today's Naval Air Reserve.

My special thanks go to the producers of this 75th Anniversary book. The writers, photographers, editors, public affairs specialists and journalists, members of the Naval Air Reserve, who spent countless off-duty hours putting the "pieces" together in order to tell this remarkable story.

I am proud of you all and prouder still to be a part of the Naval Air Reserve as it celebrates 75 years of service to the Navy and to our country.

Rear Admiral Richard K. Chambers, USNR
Commander Naval Air Reserve Force

ACKNOWLEDGMENTS

The authors would like to acknowledge the support that so many people provided to make this book possible. Captain Bill Brubaker, USNR, and Mr. Jon Lopez volunteered their writing skills to assist in the preparation of the manuscript. Many excellent and rare photographs were made available to the book by the following photographers: Commander Peter Mersky, USNR, Commander Joe Towers, USNR, Warrant Officer (1) E.O. Bailey, USNR, Chief Petty Officer R.E. Kling, USNR; Mr. George Hall, Mr. Jim Sullivan, Mr. Robert F. Dorr, and Mr. Nick Williams. Throughout the Naval Air Reserve Force, commanding officers, public affairs officers, journalists, and photographers mates spent many hours researching command histories, interviewing reservists, culling photo files, and otherwise assisting staff members in the preparation of this book. This book about the Naval Air Reserve was made possible by the efforts of the people in the Naval Air Reserve.

No less important were contributions from many organizations and people outside the Naval Air Reserve. The staffs of the Naval Aviation Historical Center and *Naval Aviation News* made available their vast and unique reference files without qualification and provided invaluable assistance to the author in his photographic and historical research. Apple Computer and the Aldus Corporation provided unsolicited technical support that greatly facilitated preparing the manuscript. Bob Lawson and the staff of *The Hook* magazine provided valuable historical information. The commanding officer of NAF Washington and his staff at the Training and Administrative Departments generously shared their facilities and manpower with the book's producers. The producers of this book are sincerely grateful to everyone who helped make this tribute to the Naval Air Reserve possible.

GLOSSARY OF ABBREVIATIONS AND ACRONYMS

ABFC	Advanced Base Functional Component.
ACDUTRA	Outdated acronym for active duty for training; usually the annual two-weeks' active duty performed by reservists.
ACM	Air Combat Maneuvering. Aerial "dogfighting."
AIMD	Aircraft Intermediate Maintenance Dept. The department that repairs test equipment and does heavier maintenance than a squadron.
ASWOC	Antisubmarine Warfare Operations Center.
AVU	Associated Volunteer Unit. Post–WW II designation for reserve established for voluntary drilling.
CNARESTRA	Chief of Naval Reserve Training. Title of the head of the reserve organization following WW II reorganization.
CNO/DCNO	Chief of Naval Operations/Deputy Chief of Naval Operations.
CV, CVN, AVT	Aircraft carrier designations. CV—conventionally powered; CVN—nuclear powered; AVT—training center.
FRS	Fleet Replacement Squadron. Active-duty squadrons that train aviators in fleet aircraft.
LTA	Lighter Than Air. Refers to dirigibles.
MAU	Master Augment Unit. A reserve unit that has its own aircraft but no mobilization billets. Members are trained in reserve aircraft but would mobilize to a fleet squadron in event of a call-up.
MMF	Mobile Maintenance Facility. A reserve unit that travels to remote sites to maintain P-3 aircraft.
NAF	Naval Air Facility. Naval Air Base that is a tenant command on another service's base.
NARTU (NARU, NAR)	Naval Air Reserve Training Unit. A reserve facility located on an active-duty base. Designation changed to NARU—Naval Air Reserve Unit—and then to NAR—Naval Air Reserve.

NAVSTA	Naval Station.
NORA	Naval Oceanographic Reserve Activity.
NORP	Naval Oceanographic Reserve Program.
NRAB	Naval Reserve Air Base. Early designation for air bases used by reserve forces. Designation later changed to NAS—Naval Air Station.
NRIP	Naval Reserve Intelligence Program.
ORE	Operations Readiness Evaluation.
RESFORON	Reserve Force Squadron. Those units that have custody of aircraft.
SAU	Squadron Augment Unit. A reserve unit with authorized flying billets but no assigned aircraft. SAUs typically fly aircraft of a parent reserve squadron or, in some cases, an active-duty replacement training squadron or fleet aircraft.
SELRES	Selected Reservist. A member of the Naval Reserve who drills with a unit but is not on active duty.
TACAIR	Tactical Air. Refers to fighter/attack communities.
TAR	Training and Administration of Reserves. A full-time active-duty Navy member who is a specialist in the reserve program.

SQUADRON DESIGNATION

HCS	Helicopter Combat Support Special
HM	Helicopter Mine Countermeasures
HS	Helicopter antisubmarine
HSL	Helicopter (ASW LAMPS squadron)
LAMPS	Light Airborne Multi-purpose System. Ship-based ASW helicopter squadron.
TACGRU	Tactical Air Control Group
TACRON	Tactical Air Control Squadron
VA	Attack
VAQ	Tactical Electronic Warfare
VAW	Airborne Early Warning
VF	Fighter
VFA	Fighter/Attack (F/A-18 squadrons)
VFC	Fighter/Composite
VP	Land-based antisubmarine patrol
VR	Transport
VS	Sea-based fixed-wing antisubmarine

AIRCRAFT ORGANIZATIONAL WINGS

CFLSW	Commander Fleet Logistics Support Wing
CHWR(HELWINGRES)	Commander Helicopter Wing Reserve
COMNAVAIRESFOR	Commander, Naval Air Reserve Force
COMNAVRESFOR	Commander, Naval Reserve Force
CRPWL(PATWINGRES)	Commander, Reserve Patrol Wing (Atlantic/Pacific)
CVWR	Reserve Carrier Air Wing

WINGS AT THE READY

THE NAVAL AIR RESERVE TODAY

The Naval Air Reserve Force has good reason to celebrate its 75th anniversary. Never in its history has it been more capable, better equipped, or more prepared for mobilization than it is today. In the event of a national emergency, our nation can call on a Naval Air Reserve force that numbers 51 squadrons, over 400 aircraft and nearly 450 aviation support units. And, unlike some times in the past, the hardware is modern and well supported. Reserve squadrons are flying modern aircraft such as the F-14 Tomcat, E-2C Hawkeye, the HH-60H Seahawk, and F/A-18 Hornet. Reserve air wings mirror active-duty air wings in organization and qualifications. Reserve pilots fly over 135 hours a year and are fully current in their tactical missions, including carrier qualifications. Individual reservists train alongside active-duty members in replacement-training squadrons and fleet squadrons to augment mobilized units as necessary. In other support roles, thousands of selected reservists serve in reinforcing and sustaining units to provide trained manpower for our aircraft carriers, naval air stations, aviation staffs, and other important components where augmenting personnel would be critical in the event of a national emergency. Clearly, our Naval Air Reserve has never been more capable of responding to national crises than it is today.

As important as this is, however, readiness to "fill the breech" is only one aspect of the reservists' mission. The role of the Naval Air Reserve has been expanded to include missions and responsibilities that go beyond the traditional mobilization role of the reserve components. As never before, the Naval Air Reserve is becoming an increasingly important part of the total defense effort as it assumes missions previously performed by active-duty forces. For example, consider just a few of the Naval Air Reserve's accomplishments in a recent year:

- Naval Air Reserve E-2, SH-2, and P-3 aircraft flew in direct support of drug-interdiction operations. This effort represented a significant part of the total navy effort devoted to this important mission.
- Reserve logistic airlift (VR) squadrons flying C-9 aircraft provided nearly all of the navy's personnel airlifts in the continental United States.
- Reserve fighter composite squadrons (VFC), flying adversary and fleet-support missions in the Douglas A-4 aircraft, provided over 10,000 flight hours in support of active navy and marine units.
- Reserve force squadrons, flying modern aircraft such as the F-14, F/A-18, and E-2C, provided over 3,000 flight hours in support of air

combat maneuvering (ACM) training, close air support, static displays, and fleet training exercises.

- Reserve helicopter squadrons provided over 2,500 hours in a variety of missions including plane guard services, SEAL team insertion/extraction, combat search and rescue, law enforcement and fleet training exercises.
- Reserve flight instructors flew over 18,000 hours to help the navy meet its annual pilot-training rate.

The Total Force concept—active and reserve forces operating together to maximize our nation's defense—is clearly the concept of the future. As defense dollars become more scarce, efficiency and economy dictate that more of the defense responsibility be passed to reserve forces. The Naval Air Reserve today is ready to assume that responsibility, thanks to the effort and resources allocated over recent years to achieve this capability. Much of the Naval Air Reserve's current success can be traced back to lessons learned from the history of the Naval Air Reserve program. As the saying goes, those who fail to learn from the mistakes of history are condemned to repeat them. On this 75th anniversary year of our Naval Air Reserve, let's look back at the roots of the reserve program to appreciate the heritage, honor those instrumental in developing a Naval Air Reserve force, and most importantly, to avoid making the same mistakes that have occurred in the past.

This formation features an E-2C, an EA-6B, an A-6E, two F/A-18s, and an F-14A of Reserve Carrier Air Wing 30. Only in recent years has the Naval Air Reserve acquired aircraft such as these that are as modern and capable as those flown by the active-duty fleet. Today, the Naval Air Reserve is a vital part of our country's total defense effort, and this capability could not have been attained without modernizing the aging equipment reserve forces had traditionally been given. *(Photo by Tom Twomey)*

An F/A-18 from VFA-303 is about to be launched off catapult one during a carrier qualification (CQ) period aboard the USS *Ranger* (CV 61). Mobilization readiness demands carrier proficiency, so annual CQ sessions are a fact of life for tactical air reservists. *(Photo by George Hall)*

An F-14 from VF-301 hurtles down the catapult in afterburner. The days of the "Weekend Warrior" have long since disappeared as reservists deploy aboard carriers, go on detachments, and devote much of their free time to reserve commitments. *(Photo by George Hall)*

An F-14A Tomcat knifes through an early-morning sky. The assignment of F-14s to the reserve forces in 1984 was a major step toward the "horizontal" integration of reserve and active forces. *(Photo by George Hall)*

An F/A-18 from VFA-303 and an F-14 from VF-301 prepare to launch from the flight deck of USS *Ranger*. Carrier operations are always demanding, but "there ain't no rookies" in Naval Air Reserve squadrons. Reserve aviators are hand-picked, and almost all come to their squadrons with many hours in aircraft type and hundreds of aircraft carrier landings. *(Photo by George Hall)*

C-9B on final approach to NAS Alameda. The VR squadrons have been one of the big success stories of the Naval Air Reserve. The transport mission proved to be ideal for the Air Reserve, and the efficiency with which reservists conducted their operations resulted in the active-duty navy transferring all its transports to the Naval Air Reserve. *(Photo by George Hall)*

Below, F/A-18 Hornets from VFA-303. The "Golden Hawks" were the first Naval Air Reserve squadron to fly the Hornet. Acceptance of the F/A-18 was another milestone for the Naval Air Reserve because it marked the first time a Naval Air Reserve squadron had ever received a new aircraft before all active-duty squadrons had transitioned to that aircraft. *(Photo by George Hall)*

The Naval Air Reserve could not have assumed the share of the VP load that it has today if its equipment had not been upgraded to fleet standards. Today reserve squadrons are flying the P-3C Update III, the latest version of the Orion, or other P-3 variants with modifications that give them the capability to hunt subs with the best of the fleet.

A C-9B from VR-57 takes time off from its busy flight schedule. Here in the squadron's hangar at North Island the unsung heroes of the Naval Air Reserve, the maintenance and maintenance support personnel, inspect the aircraft to ensure its mechanical reliability and safety.

An A-6E from VA-304 "over the ramp" during an approach to the USS *Nimitz* (CVN 68). This CQ period was the first for VA-304 flying the Intruders they accepted in the summer of 1990. The reserve carrier air wings fully mirrored their active-duty counterparts when VA-205 transitioned from the A-7E to the A-6E in 1990, giving the reserve force a medium attack capability in both airwings.

The P-3 community is probably the navy's best example of reservists and active-duty personnel working together in a common mission. Reserve Orion squadrons routinely assume active-duty patrol commitments on deployment to bases around the world. *(Photo by George Hall)*

The VP mission is shared by thirteen Naval Air Reserve squadrons, seven of which are assigned to Commander Reserve Patrol Wing Atlantic and six to Commander Reserve Patrol Wing Pacific. In addition to deploying outside of the continental United States, reserve P-3s fly both operational and training ASW (antisubmarine warfare) missions off both coasts, and in the Gulf and the Caribbean.

An E-2C prepares for an early-morning launch. The Falklands War reiterated the importance of airborne early-warning aircraft for fleet defense. With one squadron of the latest model Hawkeyes in each reserve air wing, the Naval Air Reserve has state-of-the-art radar detection capabilities. *(Photo by George Hall)*

The system is only as good as the people who operate it. For this E-2C air control officer, maintaining proficiency on the "scope" means putting in extra active duty and additional drills well beyond the one weekend a month minimum requirement. *(Photo by George Hall)*

The navy invests millions of dollars training a crew to fly a sophisticated aircraft such as the EA-6B. Retaining these experienced and expensively trained aviators in the Naval Air Reserve is a tremendous plus for the navy and our country. Continuing to fly navy aircraft offers great rewards to those aviators who love naval aviation but sought careers in the civilian world. *(Photo by George Hall)*

An EA-6B from VAQ-309 approaches the USS *Nimitz* during carquals. In this age of sophisticated missiles and anti-air defenses, electronic warfare is critical to the success of any strike mission. VAQ-309 in CVWR-30 and VAQ-209 in CVWR-20 have the latest and the best "jammer" capability. *(Photo by George Hall)*

Faces of the Naval Air Reserve: On any weekend at bases across the country, the people of the Naval Air Reserve are actively training for the major role they play in our nation's defense. While hardware is essential, the real reason for the success of the Naval Air Reserve is the men and women of today's force who make it work.

An SH-3D from HS-85 prepares to land on the deck of the USS *Independence* during a training period at sea. The reserve H-3 squadrons provide inner zone antisubmarine warfare for the aircraft carrier as well as plane guard duties during flight operations.

The rotary-wing community has developed along with the other squadrons in the Naval Air Reserve. An SH-2F from HSL-74 (top) prepares to launch from an active-duty frigate. Below, an SH-2F from HSL-84 hovers over the Pacific at sunset. Three Naval Air Reserve LAMPS (Light Airborne Multi-purpose System) squadrons, HSL 94, 84, and 74, based at NAS Willow Grove, NAS North Island, and NAS South Weymouth, respectively, give the reserve force major capability in this mission.

An A-4F from VFC-12 and an F-14 from VF-101 "at the merge". VFC-12 on the East Coast and VFC-13 on the West Coast provide a variety of aircraft services to the fleet and other reserve squadrons. Both now specialize in adversary services, a fact recognized by their redesignation in 1988 from VC to VFC. *(Photo by Peter B. Mersky)*

The HH-60H helicopter has such increased capabilities that the Naval Air Reserve was able to combine two squadron missions—HC and HAL—into one, designated HCS, Helicopter Combat Support Special. The HH-60H was the first aircraft procured specifically for the Naval Air Reserve. *(Photo by George Hall)*

The H-53 has been adapted to the mine countermeasures mission with great success. HM-18, based at NAS Norfolk, and HM-19 at NAS Alameda provide the Naval Air Reserve with a major capability in this new and important mission. *(Photo by WO1 Ed Bailey)*

The cockpit of the HH-60H glows with the latest high-tech instrumentation that enhances multi-mission performance. Relatively new to the navy, this aircraft was first delivered to HCS-5 at NAS Pt. Mugu, California, in 1989.

VFC squadrons fly the two-place TA-4J in addition to the single-seat A-4F. The "Ts" can be used for air combat maneuvering training, but are better suited for the other VC missions such as banner towing for aerial gunnery.

THE NAVAL AIR RESERVE IS BORN

Love of aviation and a desire to serve one's country have been strong motivations for naval air reservists over the years. Fittingly, it was these traits that led to the establishment of the first naval air reserve unit.

F. Trubee Davison, a sophomore at Yale University, organized what is widely considered to be the first naval air reserve unit. In the early summer of 1916, the United States appeared to be on the brink of war with Mexico. Davison and eleven other Yale students, many members of the Yale rowing crew, were enthralled with the fledgling science of flight and believed in the capability the airplane could have in the defense of their country. They had agreed that, should war break out, they would join the newly established aviation arms of the army or navy. In the meanwhile, they wanted to learn to fly.

Motivation was one thing, reality another. Acquiring an aircraft and learning to fly it, with no official funding, was a major problem. Through contacts and referrals, members of the unit were put in touch with Admiral Robert Peary, who was responsible for formulating plans for the use of navy aircraft during wartime. Admiral Peary wanted to establish a series of air stations along the East Coast, from which aircraft could patrol for submarines. Members of the Yale Unit, it was decided, could be trained as pilots for the first aerial coastal patrol unit.

Although still civilians and volunteers, the Yale students now had an official mission and reason to learn to fly. Trubee Davison was able to acquire one Curtiss "F" seaplane from Rodman Wanamaker, a New York merchant who operated a flying school in Long Island. With the airplane came one instructor, David McCulloch, who, in May 1919, would serve as copilot on one of the four NC flying boats that attempted the first transatlantic seaplane flight. With instructor and aircraft in place, the Yale Unit formed at Locust Valley, New York, during the summer of 1916 and began to learn to fly.

The summer's work actually involved a lot more than just learning to fly. Student pilots worked on engines, scrubbed down hulls, and did whatever was necessary to keep their aircraft flying. As Trubee Davison recalled, "If it had not been for the interest and enthusiasm of the pupils and their desire to labor in any way that could facilitate instruction, it would have been impossible to accomplish what we did that summer." By the end of summer, four students had soloed, and the rest were ready to do so.

The end of the summer was also significant because of some important legislation that was passed. The Naval Reserve Appropriations Act of

Here Davison was photographed next to the unit's Curtiss seaplane trainer. Flight gear of the time was anything but standard and became whatever the crew member thought appropriate and handy.

15

Yale sophomore F. Trubee Davison and eleven of this fellow students formed the First Yale Unit in August 1916. Using a Curtiss "F" seaplane contributed by Philadelphia merchant Rodman Wanamaker, the group learned to fly during the summer and by September were able to operate during naval maneuvers off the New Jersey coast. Here, Davison (third from right, rear row) poses with some members of the unit, along with their mascot, Ella.

29 August 1916 established a Naval Reserve Flying Corps. This date is considered the official birthday of the Naval Air Reserve, although some historians would claim that the birth came earlier in that summer with the organization of the Yale Unit. In any case, with the passage of this act, students in several other colleges organized flying units. Volunteer civilian units were set up in Newport News, Virginia, and Buffalo, New York, but the unit founded at Yale University is still considered the first Naval Air Reserve organization.

During the early fall of 1916, the Yale Unit students, although still civilians, took part in aerial maneuvers off Sandy Hook, New Jersey, as members of the Aerial Coastal Patrol. Davison recalled that the exercise was worthwhile from several standpoints.

"First of all, it demonstrated the value of the airplane in locating hostile ships; secondly, it proved that mines could be located far more efficiently with seaplanes than by surface craft; and thirdly, it showed the navy that civilians were not only interested in developing the aviation branch of naval warfare but were devoting their time and energy to that end."

Lieutenant John Towers, one of the navy's first active-duty aviators (Naval Aviator number three), saw the value of an air reserve and was influential in enabling the Yale Unit to join the new Naval Reserve Flying Program. On 24 March 1917, thirteen days before the United States entered World War I, the Yale Unit volunteers enlisted en masse. From this small group of twenty-nine would come a future assistant secretary of war, an assistant secretary of the navy for air, an under secretary of the navy, and a secretary of defense.

As American involvement in the war increased, the members of the Yale Unit and the other college groups were split up and sent where their expertise was needed. Many became instructors, while others went overseas to fight. In combat, members of the Naval Reserve Flying Corp established an impressive record. Among their many accomplishments the following stand out:

• Lieutenant H. T. Stanley was the first naval aviator to be credited with the destruction of a German submarine.

An early view of the Yale Unit's "air station" at Huntington Beach, Long Island, New York, in 1917. Two Curtiss seaplanes and one Curtiss R-6 floatplane are on the launch ramps.

Trubee Davison holds quarters at the Yale Unit's training station at Huntington Beach in the summer of 1917.

Members of the Yale Unit hoist their Curtiss R-6 up the ramp.

This photo of David Ingalls in a Curtiss XF8C-7 was taken when he was assistant secretary of the navy.

- Ensign Stephen Potter was the first navy pilot to shoot down an enemy seaplane.
- Lieutenant David Ingalls (a member of the First Yale Unit), flying a Sopwith Camel with the RAF, was the first naval aviator to become an ace. He would later serve as assistant secretary of the navy from 1929 to 1932.
- Ensign Charles Hammann, a member of the Naval Reserve Flying Corps, was the only naval aviator in World War I to be awarded the Congressional Medal of Honor.

Freedom is never free, however, and the Naval Reserve Flying Corps lost many fine aviators in combat. Ensign Albert Sturtevant, an original member of the Yale Unit, was the first naval aviator to give his life for his country. Tragically, Trubee Davison was never designated a naval aviator due to serious back injuries he sustained in a crash during training. Fifty years later, however, Vice Admiral Paul H. Ramsey, then DCNO (Air), pinned a set of gold wings on Davison and designated him an "Honorary Naval Aviator" in a special ceremony that coincided with the fiftieth anniversary of the Naval Air Reserve.

No less impressive than the reservists' combat record during World War I was their ability to train new pilots. A classic role of the naval reservists—to augment the regular navy during a time of emergency— was first demonstrated during World War I. In the nineteen months between the declaration of war and the time the armistice ending World War I was signed, the navy had trained more than 6,000 aviation specialists, including 2,000 aviators. At the end of the war, of the 1,656 naval aviators on duty, 1,500 were reservists. Four thousand more aviation students were undergoing training. Unfortunately, this buildup of talent would soon be decimated.

It would take another world war before policymakers would take to heart the importance of maintaining a ready reserve. As one observer noted, "The last chorus of 'Over There' faded into the din of the victory cheers, and Americans did not recognize their new heritage of international responsibility—they sought a rapid return to pre-war isolation. Mass demobilization was what the nation wanted." And that's what they

David Ingalls with Will Rogers.

Many of the original reserve naval aviators served in ASW units at French coastal installations. Here six young crewmen pose rather informally by their Curtiss HS-1 at Treguir in 1918. Their uniforms are the precursors of aviation greens and show a wide variety of personal choice.

Alexander McCormick, a member of the Second Yale Unit, is pictured in flight gear of the era.

U.S. Navy pilots at Killingholme, England, in July of 1918. Unfortunately, there is no record of the names of those who assembled for this rare photo.

got. In less than a year, more than 24,000 officers and 286,000 enlisted men were released from active duty. The 500 reserve officers remaining in the navy became regulars. Having just won the "war to end all wars," there was little public support to maintain a large military force, let alone a reserve flying organization. Starved for financial and public support, the Naval Reserve Flying Corps was virtually inactive by the end of 1922. Fortunately, a few men of vision had the courage and wisdom to buck prevailing opinion and fight for the Naval Air Reserve. Rear Admiral William Moffett was one.

A NAVAL AVIATION RESERVE POLICY IS ESTABLISHED

Admiral Moffett was convinced that a reserve establishment was imperative for the nation's defense. He personally developed a comprehensive plan to re-establish the Naval Reserve Flying Corps and used his considerable powers of persuasion to seek approval from the chief of naval operations. On 16 November 1923, a definitive naval aviation reserve policy based on Moffett's proposal was approved. The policy provided for "one unit" (two planes plus 50 percent spares) in each naval district where "public interest and condition warrant." Each unit was responsible for training ten new pilots a year. Formally, their mission was defined as "the enrollment and training of new members who were suitable officer material in order to ensure a supply of new blood; and to maintain the efficiency of members already qualified."

Bases were immediately established at Squantum, Massachusetts (just outside of Boston), Great Lakes, Illinois, and Fort Hamilton, New York. Two years later a "two-unit" base was established at Sand Point (Seattle),

Washington. Thirty-three students qualified in primary training at Squantum in 1923 and were given forty-five days of advanced training the following year at Hampton Roads, Virginia. This training included navigation, gunnery, and bombing along with ground training in the theory of flight. While undergoing their flight training, the students were designated naval aviation student pilots and were given the rating of seamen second class. At the successful conclusion of their training, and after having passed a professional examination, they were commissioned ensigns, class five, U.S. Naval Reserve Force. They were also designated as naval aviators.

The reserve received another shot in the arm with the passage of the Naval Reserve Act of 1925. This was the most comprehensive reserve legislation enacted up to that time. It defined compulsory reserve service, reduced the number of classes of reservists to three instead of six, and outlined drill pay, appointments, retirements, and periods of active duty. It completely federalized whatever state naval militias still existed, requiring 95 percent of its members to be enrolled in the U.S. Naval Reserve. It also provided a uniform syllabus for training for all units, including ground and flight instruction.

One of the more unusual aircraft used by student naval aviators was this Burgess-Dunne floatplane, seen here on the ramp at Pensacola. The aircraft's engine and propeller were mounted amidships. Reservists who successfully finished elimination training completed their flight instruction at Pensacola.

In March 1926, the Navy Department adopted a five-year plan for training aviation reservists, including enlisted members. Until then, virtually no provision had been made for training enlisted reservists in their critical aviation roles. This new plan mandated that every reservist would obtain at least four hours of training each month along with two weeks of active duty per year. The individual reservist would be assigned to a specific squadron and would receive training geared toward mobilization. The Naval Air Reserve was back in business.

Curtiss trainers, usually configured as floatplanes, were widely used early naval aircraft. The series were equipped with a variety of engines—whatever was available—and did yeoman service, not only as flight trainers, but as occasional antisubmarine patrol aircraft, carrying small bombs and one or two light machine guns. This Curtiss N-9 trainer at moorings is equipped with the Hispano Suiza engine.

The Naval Reserve Air Base at Sand Point, Washington, was authorized two years after Squantum. The base, situated on Lake Washington only a few miles from downtown Seattle, was constructed on one of the city's early golf courses.

Above, facilities in the early days of naval aviation were marginal at best, but level ground and temporary shelter were sufficient to sustain operations. The ramp and "hangars" at NRAB Sand Point, Washington, are shown in this early twenties photograph.

A Vought UO-1 on the ramp at NRAB Squantum, 1926. Among the first aircraft allocated for reserve use, the Vought saw service not only as a mount for reservists but also as an enforcer of Prohibition, flying along the New England coast watching for rum-runner activities. *(Courtesy of Peter B. Mersky)*

Naval Air Reservists start a trainer at Squantum. NRAB Squantum was one of the three original "two unit" Naval Reserve Air Bases established in the early '20s. *(Courtesy of Peter B. Mersky)*

CONTINUED GROWTH

The remainder of the twenties saw continued growth in the Naval Air Reserve. New bases opened up at Oakland, California, Grosse Ile, Michigan, Minneapolis, Minnesota, Anacostia, Maryland, near Washington, D.C., and Long Beach, California. Every reserve squadron had NY-2 aircraft, and new O2U-1 biplanes were arriving in the inventory. The aircraft were maintained by "stationkeepers," full-time naval personnel assigned to the NRABs. The mission of the NRABs was threefold: to enroll new members for flight training; to provide elimination training for prospective naval aviators; and lastly, to offer facilities and training for already qualified naval reserve pilots so that they might maintain their proficiency. Elimination flight training weeded out approximately 50 percent of the candidates, but the successful students went on to advanced training. Advanced training was done at the NRABs until 1928 when that function was transferred to Pensacola, Florida. After advanced training and commissioning, students then served with a fleet squadron for one year as an ensign, USNR, Class A-V(G), and then went to inactive status with an aviation fleet division of the reserve to maintain their proficiency through weekly and annual drills.

By the end of the decade, Admiral Moffett pushed through another program that provided for five additional squadrons, a force of 186 reserve aircraft and a total of twelve reserve air bases. The Naval Air Reserve had come a long way in seven years.

The thirties were a "mixed bag" for the reserve. Building on the momentum established in the late twenties, the reserve enjoyed a successful period early in the decade. The reserve air bases were developing

NRAB Minneapolis was one of several new reserve bases established in the late '20s. Minneapolis provided a training and proficiency flying site for naval air reservists in the Midwest.

NAS Anacostia reservists return from a mission in their Vought UO-1. Note the admiral's pennant on the inner-bay wing strut. Located in Washington, D.C., Anacostia served many requirements, occasionally providing transportation for high-ranking navy officials. Reserve bases at Anacostia, Minneapolis, Oakland, Grosse Ile, and Long Beach were established under a five-year plan implemented in the late '20s for the Naval Air Reserve.

The establishment of NRAB Long Beach in 1928 marked the beginning of a long history of Naval Air Reserve activity in southern California.

systematic and progressive methods for training officers and enlisted while service-type aircraft were being procured and delivered to the reserve forces. The National Relief Administration agencies helped improve base facilities by enlarging runways and providing night-flying capabilities. Navy and marine reservists in turn carried out mosquito abatement and search-and-rescue and photo-mapping flights for several agencies. In 1931 the reservists flew more than 26,000 hours with no fatalities. Unfortunately, the economic distresses brought about by the Great Depression of 1929 eventually filtered down to the Naval Air Reserve, and funding was drastically reduced during 1933 and 1934. Annual flight time for aviators was cut to forty-five hours, a number clearly inadequate to maintain their proficiency. Drill attendance became largely voluntary. In 1934 only fourteen aviators would receive commissions in the Naval Reserve.

THE ROLE OF THE RESERVE IS DEFINED

Fortunately, the Federal Aviation Commission, appointed in 1934 to study and make recommendations on all phases of aviation, recognized these deficiencies in the reserve program. The commission's recommendation No. 54 addressed the aviation reserve and called for a "higher priority in the allotment of funds for the aviation reserve of both the Navy and Army." The recommendation also defined the role of the aviation reserve and suggested that its numbers be greatly increased. The recommendation established a basic philosophy that would exist for years and read, in part:

"In war against a major power, our air forces would feel an almost instant need for the mobilization of at least twice their regular personnel. The numbers immediately mobilized in full readiness for duty would have to be backed up, in order that military effort could be carried on, by a reserve of some additional thousands of qualified pilots who could be made ready for full service within a few weeks. As we have studied the present status of the reserve, it has seemed to us that this problem has been faced on so small a scale as scarcely to constitute more than a working model. The Navy has a total enrolled reserve of 481 officer pilots, of whom 251 could be considered as ready for immediate duty. It seems to us conservative to say that the aggregate of effective air force reserves should be at least double what it is now. The specific need here seems to be for additional funds for reserve purposes."

RESERVE CATEGORIES AND DESIGNATIONS IN THE THIRTIES

In 1934 the Naval Reserve was made up of three categories: the Fleet Naval Reserve, the Merchant Marine Naval Reserve and the Volunteer Naval Reserve. The first and third categories included aviation personnel. The Fleet Naval Reserve consisted of officers and men in training or qualified for combat duty. The designation of aviation officers in this category was A-F. There was no designation for aeronautically affiliated enlisted men.

The Volunteer Naval Reserve was made up of officers and men available for assignment in the event of war but for whom drills and training were voluntary. There were two subdivisions of the VNR: individuals qualified for combat and designated for general service (G); and individuals available for specific duties and as technical specialists (engineers, attorneys, physicians), designated (S) . The first group included reserve officers who had served in World War I, former navy officers and naval aviators. All of these individuals were eligible to be members of the Fleet Naval Reserve, but lack of vacancies in squadrons and the distance to meetings precluded membership in this group. Officers of the Voluntary Reserve available for general aviation service were designated A-V(G). Aviation officers available for special service carried an A-V(K) designation, supply officers were designated A-V(S), and transport pilots, A-V(T).

Unlike the Fleet Naval Reserve, the volunteer reserve did identify enlisted personnel who were associated with aviation. Volunteer enlisteds affiliated with aviation were in the V-2 classification, while student naval aviators were classified as V-5 until they were commissioned.

EARLY SQUADRON DESIGNATIONS AND AIRCRAFT MARKINGS

The first units of the Naval Air Reserve were designated as fixed-wing training squadrons (VN). Aircraft assigned to the reserve force were identified by an "R" following the squadron number, and then another number behind a "D" that corresponded to the naval district to which the squadron was assigned. Thus, squadron VN-3RD3 would be Reserve Training Squadron Three, assigned to the Third Naval District, since the squadron was based at New York.

Early reserve aircraft were marked in a variety of ways. Some had the name of the base they were attached to painted on the side of their aircraft along with the ship number. Others carried the squadron designation code with the ship number attached to the end. Thus, VN-13RD11-2 would identify the second aircraft assigned to Reserve Training Squadron 13 at Long Beach, California (Naval District 11). An aircraft identified by a code such as VN-3-4RD3 would indicate that it was flown by two reserve training squadrons, 3 and 4, assigned to a base in the Third Naval District.

Other marking variations on reserve aircraft included the letters USNR or NRAB followed by the base where the aircraft was assigned: USNR NAS Anacostia, for example. Some squadrons developed their own unique logos and affixed them to the aircraft. The Golden Gaters of

An O2C-1 is parked on the ramp at Great Lakes, Illinois. Air operations in the Chicago area moved to Glenview before the outbreak of World War II.

Oakland, California, were one example, while one Anacostia-based squadron had a small Washington Monument painted on its aircraft.

During the thirties, some squadrons painted their vertical stabilizers a solid color to identify their base. The color codes were as follows:

NRAB Long Beach	black
NRAB Great Lakes	red
NRAB Seattle	green
NRAB New York	blue
NRAB Grosse Ile	red
NRAB Oakland	green

In July of 1937, all reserve squadrons were redesignated scouting squadrons, and the naval district number was dropped from the squadron designation. For example, Reserve Squadron 13 based at Long Beach, California, changed its designation from VN-13RD11 to VS-13R.

THE AVIATION CADET PROGRAM

The Aviation Cadet Act of 1935 was another important program that resulted from the Federal Aviation Commission's recommendations. This program was designed to help both the active-duty forces and the reserve. Under the program, college graduates entered active duty as aviation cadets, were trained to fly, and then served with the fleet until their four-year commitment was up. At that time they would be commissioned as ensigns in the Naval Reserve, where they would form a pool of experienced pilots who could be used in times of emergency. Cadets were paid $75 per month during flight training and $125 per month while on active duty. Despite what appears to be meager compensation by today's standards, the cadet program was a success. Fifty-five cadets started training on 20 July 1935, and by September, 192 cadets were in training. Two hundred and one other cadets were being screened for the program through a process called "elimination training," conducted at reserve

Pre–World War II elimination flight training, a part of the Aviation Cadet Program, was a major reserve responsibility. Here, at NAS Minneapolis, N3Ns begin taxiing for a training flight. Cadets who proved their aeronautical ability during the elimination phase of training were sent on to complete their flight instruction at Pensacola.

bases. Cadets who proved their aeronautic adaptability by passing this training then reported to Pensacola, Florida, for the duration of their training. By 1938, 526 cadets were flying with the fleet.

The cadet program, while successful, did not produce the numbers of reserve pilots that planners deemed necessary. Some of the pilots stayed on active duty, and the total number of pilots trained was simply not sufficient to meet the needs of the active and reserve forces. The annual report of the chief of the Bureau of Navigation for fiscal year 1939 stated that the shortage of qualified pilots in the reserve aviation

In addition to elimination flight training, reserve bases in the mid-1930s were responsible for providing proficiency and currency training for already designated aviators. The O2C-1s shown above were used for both training and proficiency.

A radioman-gunner checks his machine gun's ammunition.

squadrons "has long been a matter of concern to the Bureau." The Bureau of Aeronautics agreed that immediate action to remedy the deficiency in reserve personnel was necessary. They proposed to increase the number of cadets in training by 350 over fleet needs and to commission private and commercial pilots not employed by the airlines. These pilots would receive further training at naval reserve aviation bases while on active duty and then would be incorporated into reserve squadrons as naval aviators. Unfortunately, these and other recommendations languished in the bureaucracy and no action was taken. When the United States entered World War II in 1941, only about 600 aviators and 700 enlisted reservists could be counted as immediately available.

A group of Minneapolis reservists check their Grumman's landing gear in the mid-1930s.

One of the last types to serve with the Naval Air Reserve before World War II was the Curtiss SBC Helldiver, one of the last biplanes in naval service. Here, an SBC-4 from NRAB Oakland waits on the ramp. Stationed at the base between 1939–40, these aircraft were eventually transferred to France under the Lend-Lease Program, making their way, under the cover of darkness, to Canada. However, the fall of France in June 1940 halted further shipment, and the type served with Canadian training units.

WORLD WAR II

As in World War I, the navy's ability to build its aviation training capability, in large part through reserve facilities, was truly staggering. For example, prior to the start of World War II a total of 1,800 aviation cadets had been trained. In 1941, the input rate jumped to 7,000 and by the end of 1943, the rate soared to 20,000 per year! To facilitate this massive training effort, the reserve opened major new bases at New Orleans, Atlanta, and Dallas and greatly expanded training at the existing NRABs. By the end of the war in August 1945, reservists on active duty made up 83 percent of the navy's fleet manpower.

The training program facilitated by the reserve establishment turned out thousands of pilots, but this did not mean that the standards for obtaining the "Wings of Gold" were compromised whatsoever. The training program was long and arduous, testing the fortitude and motivation of the candidates as it has done for generations of naval aviation students before and after.

For many who enlisted during World War II in the Naval Reserve to become pilots, the Civilian Pilot Training Program was the path to the wings of gold. It was a four-step process. In the first phase, or elimination program, the candidates learned to fly in the tiny Piper Cub from fields across the country. If they succeeded in passing this hurdle, they moved on to advanced preflight where they received indoctrination in navy customs and traditions and much close-order drilling.

Step three was primary flight school at one of the naval air stations, most likely a former Naval Reserve Air Base (NRABs were designated NAS's in 1943). Here volunteer reserve instructors trained students in the N3N "Yellow Peril," an open-cockpit biplane considerably larger than the Cub. Aerobatic flying plus day and night courses prepared students for the final, advanced phase of training at Pensacola, Florida. There, after instrument flying, gunnery, and courses in over-water navigation,

Training was a major role for the Naval Air Reserve during World War II. Pictured above is the flightline at NAS Atlanta, one of three major new reserve air bases established to train naval aviators during the war.

the student pilots received their wings. It was a sixteen-month process, if all went well.

After designation, the new aviators were assigned to the aircraft that they would fly in the fleet. Those selected for fighter aircraft might continue training at NAS Jacksonville, Florida, while those destined for bombers would go to bases like NAS Deland, Florida. The volume of needed training was such that many cities with suitable runways were pressed into service. Vero Beach, Fort Lauderdale, Miami, and Key West were typical cities where intensive flight training sprung up during the war years.

The massive training effort paid off. Once again, the ability to expand existing forces in a time of crisis through the use of a reserve force proved its worth. The defeat of the Axis Powers could not have been accomplished without naval air reservists.

HISTORY MAKERS OF THE NAVAL AIR RESERVE

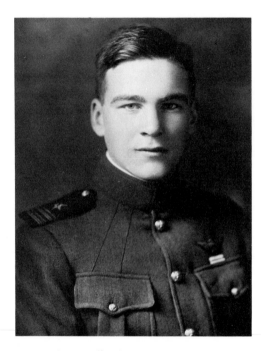

Lt. David S. Ingalls, the navy's first ace.

David Sinton Ingalls, USNR

David Sinton Ingalls, United States Naval Reserve Force, holds a prominent place in the history of the Naval Air Reserve. Born in Cleveland, Ohio, on 29 January 1899, Ingalls entered Yale University in 1916. There he met F. Trubee Davison and immediately enrolled in the First Yale Unit, a group of students who formed a flying club to learn how to fly. The Yale Unit eventually became part of the Naval Reserve Force in 1917, and all its members volunteered for active duty. Training in seaplanes at West Palm Beach, Florida, and Huntington, New York, Lieutenant Ingalls qualified as Naval Aviator (heavier than air) # 85 in August 1917. He was promoted to ensign in September, and along with six other members of the Yale Unit, sailed for England and combat in World War I on 23 September 1917.

After some additional training in England and France, Ingalls was assigned to the British Royal Air Force Squadron 213. In August and September of 1918, Ingalls, flying a Sopwith Camel, was credited with shooting down at least four enemy aircraft and one balloon. He thus became the first—and only—navy ace of World War I.

He left Squadron 213 in October of the same year and served as a ferry pilot and instructor at Eastleigh, England, for the duration of the war. For his war efforts he was awarded the Distinguished Service Medal, the French Legion of Honor, and the British Distinguished Flying Cross. The last portion of the recommendation for this award reads:

His keenness, courage and utter disregard for his personal safety are exceptional and are an example to all. He is one of the finest men this squadron ever had.

/s/ Major Ronald Graham, commanding officer, No. 213 Squadron, Royal Air Force

After the war Lieutenant Ingalls re-entered Yale and received an A.B. degree in 1920. He then earned a law degree in 1923 and practiced law in Cleveland until 1929. He was elected to the Ohio legislature where he co-sponsored the Aviation Code Act of Ohio and helped design the Cleveland Airport. President Hoover, attracted by Ingalls's outstanding reputation, appointed him as assistant secretary of the navy for aeronautics. He was also appointed a lieutenant commander in the Naval Reserve while in the Navy Department.

Following the outbreak of World War II, Ingalls reported for active duty as assistant operations officer on the staff of the commander, Naval Air Force, U.S. Pacific. He served tours as executive officer, forward area and air center commander at Guadalcanal; plans observer, South Pacific Force; and commanding officer, NAS Hawaii, where he was awarded the Bronze Star.

After retiring from the navy as a rear admiral, Ingalls was vice president of Pan-American World Airways and later president of the Cleveland *Times Star.* Rear Admiral Ingalls was enshrined in the National Aviation Hall of Fame, Dayton, Ohio, in 1983. He died after suffering a stroke at the age of eighty-six at his home in Chagrin Falls, Ohio.

Charles H. Hammann, USNR

Ensign Charles Hazeltine Hammann, United States Naval Reserve Force, was the first American airman to be awarded the Congressional Medal of Honor. Ensign Hammann was born in Baltimore, Maryland, in 1892 and enlisted in the navy in October 1917.

Hammann wanted to get into aviation, and the opportunity came to him in an unusual fashion. In early 1918, the Italian and U.S. governments reached an agreement whereby the U.S. Navy would take over and operate an Italian air station at Porto Corsini, about fifty miles south of Venice. As part of the arrangement, the Italians agreed to provide flight training and aircraft for the American fliers.

Hammann and seventy-two other U.S. servicemen were selected for the program and began ground and flight training on 21 February 1918 at the Naval Flying School in Bolsena, Italy, fifty miles northeast of Rome. The school was under the direction of Ensign W. B. Atwater, but most of the courses were taught by Italians. Likewise, aircraft maintenance and ground support were arranged through a special draft of mechanics selected from men training at the various Italian seaplane and engine factories.

The air station at Porto Corsini officially came under U.S. control on 24 July 1918. Porto Corsini was located in a strategic position in relation to Pola, Austria-Hungary, the site of a major enemy naval base. Battleships and cruisers of the High Seas Fleet were anchored at Pola, and German and Austrian submarines came and went from this port during their patrols. Pola was clearly a major target for both U.S. and Italian aviators.

The planes the navy used at Porto Corsini were Italian Macchi M-5s and M-8s. The M-8s were two-seater flying boats capable of carrying four 24-pound bombs and one machine gun. The M-5 aircraft were single-seat flying boats equipped with two machine guns and designed as fighters.

On 21 August 1918, the station at Porto Corsini carried out its first mission. Five fighters and two bombers set out on a mission to drop propaganda leaflets across the Adriatic Sea near the Pola Naval Base. Fifteen minutes into the flight, one of the bombers and one of the fighters had to turn back due to engine problems. That left one bomber and four fighters. Piloting two of the fighters were Ensigns George Ludlow and Charles Hammann.

The attack group arrived over the target around 1120 on the 18th. The bomber jettisoned its leaflets from 8,000 feet while the fighters orbited overhead at 12,000 feet looking for enemy aircraft. They didn't have to wait long. Five Albatross-type fighters scrambled in pursuit of the Macchis, and Ensign Ludlow gave the signal for his division to attack.

In the ensuing dogfight, Ensign Ludlow's aircraft was hit and went into a diving spiral. He managed to pull out of the spin just prior to impact and make a semi-controlled crash into the water five miles offshore. Looking down, Hammann could see Ludlow's wrecked aircraft and the survivor on the wing. He decided to attempt a rescue.

This was a daring move for several reasons. The wind was blowing at

20 miles per hour, making a water landing hazardous. To further complicate things, Hammann's aircraft had been damaged in the dogfight, possibly precluding a takeoff even if a safe landing could be made. Finally, the aircraft was close to the harbor, making Hammann and Ludlow sitting ducks for any enemy aircraft that were still in the vicinity.

Undeterred by these considerations, Hammann spiraled down and landed beside Ludlow's crippled aircraft. Ludlow kicked holes in his Macchi to make it sink faster and then jumped onto Hammann's plane. He climbed up behind the pilot's seat and held onto the struts to keep from being swept overboard.

The Macchi M-5 was built to carry only one man. Hammann had no idea how he was going to get the overloaded aircraft airborne with a damaged hull, but somehow he did. As a final act of heroism, Hammann made another pass over the downed aircraft to fire his remaining machine-gun rounds into the hull so that the abandoned aircraft would not fall into enemy hands.

Hammann limped back to Porto Corsini, fortunately unnoticed by enemy fighters. The pilot made a good landing in the canal at Porto Corsini, but water poured through the damaged bow of the aircraft and it flipped over. Both pilots were rescued, injured but alive.

The Italian government awarded the Silver Medal of Valor to Ensign Hammann for his heroism. Shortly thereafter, Ensign Hammann was awarded the Medal of Honor for heroism "above and beyond the call of duty" in his rescue of a fellow airman.

Tragically, Ensign Hammann was killed in the crash of a Macchi flying boat at Langley Field, Virginia, about a year later. A destroyer named for him, the USS *Hammann* (DD 412), was launched in 1939. This ship was sunk in the battle of Midway, but another ship, a destroyer escort (DE 131) was named in honor of America's first aviator to win the Medal of Honor—and a reserve aviator at that.

Noel Davis, USNR

Noel Davis was one of the early leaders in Naval Aviation Reserve history. He actually began his navy career as a regular navy surface officer, graduating from the U.S. Naval Academy in 1912. During World War I, he distinguished himself on the staff of Admiral Joseph Strauss as an expert on minelaying. After the armistice ending World War I was signed, he again distinguished himself by developing techniques to safely sweep up the mines that remained from the war effort. Davis is also credited with developing techniques for navy gun spotting.

With the war over, Davis became enthralled with the growing world of aviation and entered flight training at Pensacola, Florida, attaining designation in 1922. He then took leave from the navy to pursue a law degree at Harvard University. During the three years that he studied at Harvard, he commanded the Squantum Naval Air Reserve Field. His performance as commanding officer was so outstanding that Davis returned to Washington as the head of all Naval Reserve flying operations after completing his law degree at Harvard.

During his time as the head of reserve flying, Noel Davis was an enthusiastic promoter of the Naval Air Reserve and was able to obtain additional funding and aircraft for the fledgling organization. Additionally, working at night, he developed an airplane sextant that was proclaimed to be state of the art for the 1920s. He planned to use this sextant to navigate in a flight from New York to Paris.

Lieutenant Commander Davis got the idea of flying to Paris when the Frenchman, René Fonck, began making highly visible preparations to fly from New York to Paris and win a $25,000 prize. Davis immediately rose to

Lt. Noel Davis was Squantum's second CO. He was killed in a plane crash in 1927 while preparing for a New York–Paris flight. A trophy bearing his name is awarded annually to the best Naval Air Reserve squadrons in various mission categories.

the challenge of having U.S. aircraft and engines, rather than foreign equipment, succeed on this difficult mission. Using a large, triple-motored American Legion biplane, Noel Davis began preparations for his transatlantic trip.

Tragically, Lieutenant Commander Noel Davis was killed while testing his large biplane at the high gross weights that would be necessary to carry the required fuel. He took off from Langley Field, Virginia, at a gross weight of 17,000 pounds. The airplane struggled into the air but had to turn to miss some trees off the end of the runway. The biplane lost altitude in the turn and crashed in a marshy area. Both Davis and his copilot were killed.

Noel Davis, born on Christmas Day in 1891 (hence his name), died at the age of thirty-five. His efforts on behalf of Naval Reserve Aviation were truly significant and have not been forgotten. Every year the best squadron in the Naval Air Reserve receives the coveted Noel Davis Trophy.

Jack Shea, USNR

One of the legendary figures of the early Naval Air Reserve was Commander Jack Shea of Boston, Massachusetts. Commissioned an ensign at the close of WW I, Shea returned to civilian life and joined the Aviation Reserve Division at Naval Reserve Air Base (NRAB) Squantum, Massachusetts. He eventually became executive officer of Squantum and remained there until 1940. Like thousands of other fellow reservists, Commander Shea was recalled to active duty in 1940, reporting aboard the USS *Wasp* as air operations officer. The *Wasp* was destined to see heavy action after Pearl Harbor, fighting with the few American aircraft carriers operational in the Pacific early in the war. The responsibility to face the seemingly invincible Japanese naval war machine and halt the enemy drive across the Pacific fell to this small band of forward-based ships.

The USS *Wasp* fought heroically to stem the tide of the advancing Japanese fleet, which was eventually stopped, and America slowly regained the offensive. While supporting the U.S. invasion of Guadalcanal in the late summer of 1942, however, the *Wasp* was sunk and Commander Shea was reported "missing in action." Shea was well known throughout his command as a hard-working and dedicated naval officer, but his fame in the "outside" world came through a letter that he wrote to his five-year-old son, Jackie, just before he sailed on *Wasp*'s final cruise in June 1942. Shea's letter became a classic and is reproduced below:

Dear Jackie:

This is the first letter I have written directly to my little son. I am thrilled to know that you can read it all by yourself. If you miss some of the words it will be because I do not write very plainly. Mother will help you in that case, I am sure.

I was certainly glad to hear your voice over the long-distance telephone. It sounded as though I were right in the living room with you. You sounded as though you missed your daddy very much. I miss you, too, more than anyone will ever know. It is too bad this war could not have been delayed a few more years so that I could have grown up again with you and do all the things I planned to do when you were old enough to go to school.

I thought how nice it would be to come home early in the afternoon and play ball with you and go mountain climbing and see the trees and brooks, and learn all about woodcraft, hunting, fishing, swimming and other things like that. I suppose we must be brave and put these things off now for a while.

Commander John J. Shea, for whom Shea Field at both NAS Squantum and NAS South Weymouth were named, as he appeared shortly before his death in 1942 while serving as air operations officer on board the USS *Wasp* (CV 7). He was executive officer of NAS Squantum when ordered to the Pacific. The *Wasp* was sunk on 15 September 1942, and Commander Shea was last seen that day fighting a fire on the flight deck.

When you are a little bigger you will know why your daddy is not home so much any more. You know we have a big country and we have ideas as to how people should live and enjoy the riches of it and how each is born with equal rights to life, freedom and pursuit of happiness. Unfortunately, there are some countries in the world where they do not have these ideas, where a boy cannot grow up to be what he wants to be with no limit on his opportunities to be a great man, such as a great priest, statesman, soldier, businessman, etc.

Because there are people in countries who want to change our nation, its ideals, its form of government and way of life, we must leave our homes and families to fight. Fighting for the defense of our country is an honor and a duty which your daddy has to do before he can come home and settle down with you and mother. When it is done he is coming home to be with you always and forever. So wait just a little while longer. I am afraid it will be more than the two weeks you told me on the phone.

In the meantime, take good care of Mother, be a good boy and grow up to be a good young man. Study hard when you go to school. Be a leader in everything good in life. Be a good Catholic and you can't help being a good American. Play fair always. Strive to win but if you lose, lose like a gentleman and a good sportsman.

Don't ever be a quitter, either in sports or in your business or profession when you grow up. Get all the education you can. Stay close to Mother and follow her advice. Obey her in everything, no matter how you may at times disagree. She knows what is best and will never let you down or lead you away from the right and honorable things in life.

If I don't get back, you will have to be Mother's protector because you will be the only one she has. You must grow up to take my place as well as your own in her life and heart.

Love your grandmother and granddad as long as they live. They, too, will never let you down. Love your aunts and see them as often as you can. Last of all, don't ever forget your daddy. Pray for him to come back, and if it is God's will that he does not, be the kind of a boy and man your daddy wants you to be.

Kiss Mother for me every night. Goodbye for now.

With all my love and devotion for Mother and you, Your Daddy."

The letter gives a good feeling for the commitment many reservists felt during their period of active service. The airfield at NAS South Weymouth, a descendant of NRAB Squantum, is named in honor of Jack Shea.

George Bush, USNR

George Herbert Walker Bush, 41st president of the United States, was also a distinguished Naval Air Reserve pilot. After graduating from high school at Phillips Academy in Andover, Massachusetts, in 1941, Bush enlisted in the United States Naval Reserve as a seaman 2nd class. He was commissioned an ensign following flight training at Minneapolis, MN, and Corpus Christi, TX, and was reportedly the youngest designated naval aviator for a time. He served for three years with the Third and Fifth Fleets flying TBM Avenger bombers.

In September 1944, Lieutenant (j.g.) Bush was shot down while attacking a radio tower on Chichi Jima, an island in the Bonin chain. The Japanese had established a powerful radio transmitter on Chichi, and through it the Japanese Air Command was receiving critical information about the flight routes of American air missions launched from Saipan and Tinian. Flying off

George Bush smiles in relief after he had to ditch his Avenger in the sea. He was quickly picked up, along with his two crewmen, by the destroyer *Bronson*. (*Courtesy of the White House*)

the light aircraft carrier USS *San Jacinto*, Lieutenant (j.g.) Bush led a flight of four Avengers from VT-51 against the radio station. The attacks were opposed by intense antiaircraft fire. Lieutenant (j.g.) Bush's aircraft was hit while in its dive, but the pilot completed the run and dropped two 500-pound bombs on target before limping out to sea. Bush's two crewmen were killed instantly, and the aircraft was burning badly. Lieutenant (j.g.) Bush bailed out 1,000 to 2,000 feet over the water.

After what he describes as "four terrifying hours in the water," Lieutenant (j.g.) Bush was rescued by the submarine USS *Finback*. Although the downed pilot was most happy to be rescued, he had to spend thirty days aboard the *Finback* while it completed its combat cruise. Bush recalls that the numerous depth-charge attacks the submarine endured were every bit as harrowing as flying into enemy antiaircraft fire. Finally, after thirty days at sea, the rescued pilot reached Pearl Harbor and began some much needed R&R.

For his heroism during the war, Lieutenant Bush was awarded three Air Medals and a Distinguished Flying Cross. The citation for his DFC reads as follows:

> For heroism and extraordinary achievement in aerial flight as pilot of a Torpedo Plane in Torpedo Squadron Fifty One, attached to USS *San Jacinto*, in action against enemy Japanese forces in the vicinity of the Bonin Islands on September 2, 1944. Leading one section of a four-plane division in a strike against a radio station, Ltjg Bush pressed home an attack in the face of intensive anti-aircraft fire. Although his plane was hit and set afire at the beginning of the dive, he continued his plunge toward the target and succeeded in scoring damaging bomb hits before bailing out of the craft. His courage and devotion to duty were in keeping with the highest traditions of the United States Naval Service.

Lieutenant (j.g.) Bush finished his service with tours in VT-97 and VT-153 and was released from active duty in September 1945. He enrolled at Yale University and graduated Phi Beta Kappa in economics. Mr. Bush worked in the oil industry after his graduation from Yale and eventually founded Zapata Off-Shore Oil Company. Under his direction the company became a multi-million dollar corporation. Mr. Bush entered politics in 1959 and has served the United States as a congressman, senator, permanent representative to the U.N., chief of the U.S. Liaison Office in the People's Republic of China, director of the CIA, vice president and president of the United States.

President Bush is typical of the thousands of reservists who have served their country proudly and well as both a Naval Reservist and a citizen.

A NEW ERA FOR THE NAVAL AIR RESERVE

The lessons learned from demobilization after World War I were not lost on navy planners following World War II. The navy was determined that the large pool of trained and experienced aviators standing down from the war should be retained in a reserve status. To accomplish this goal, the Naval Air Reserve Training Command was established at Glenview, Illinois, on 1 November 1945. Many of the air stations that had been established or enlarged to accommodate the World War II training load were transferred to the control of the Chief of Naval Air Reserve. Included in this group were the following bases:

New Orleans	Memphis	Los Alamitos
St. Louis	Willow Grove	Grosse Ile
Minneapolis	Atlanta	Olathe
Squantum	Dallas	Columbus
New York	Livermore	Glenview

Additionally, Naval Air Reserve Training Units (NARTUs) were established at active-duty bases at Anacostia, Norfolk, Jacksonville, Miami, Seattle, and San Diego. In 1947, air stations at Denver, Colorado, Akron, Ohio, and Louisville, Kentucky, were established along with a NARTU at Lakehurst, New Jersey.

A new concept, the associated volunteer unit (AVU), came into being about this time to further accommodate drilling reservists. The AVUs were established at various locations where non-pay reservists could come for regular drills. Aviation AVUs, designated AVU(a), conducted flight training at local municipal airports using aircraft from affiliated reserve air stations. These bases were known as Naval Air Reserve Auxiliaries and included sites such as Hutchinson, Kansas; Fresno, California; Tampa, Florida; Salt Lake City, Utah; Spokane, Washington; Phoenix, Arizona; Grand Rapids, Michigan; and Reno, Nevada.

By 1949, the Naval Air Reserve had drilling sites accessible to pilots all across the country. A variety of programs existed tailored to the desires of the individual, but all with the "bottom line" of keeping veteran pilots affiliated with the Naval Air Reserve.

Pilots in the "organized" reserve were authorized pay billets and scheduled for one hundred hours of flight time a year. Pilots in the AVU(a) units received fifty hours of flight time. CNARESTRA had trouble filling the quotas in the first few years after the war, but by 1947 the reserve forces could muster 4,907 aviators and 15,738 enlisted men. They

Following WW II, Minneapolis, like most Naval Reserve Air Bases, changed its primary mission from basic training to proficiency training. Aviators seasoned by wartime experience in WW II affiliated with reserve units and "stayed current" across the country flying aircraft such as this TBM-3E. *(Courtesy of Jim Sullivan)*

flew and maintained 2,051 aircraft including the F6F-5, F4U-4, PBY-5A, and the SNB. Training was realistic and extensive, including carrier qualifications. In November 1948, Dallas-based squadrons carrier-qualified aboard the USS *Wright*, the first carrier qualifications conducted since the end of the war. In 1949, Carrier Air Group 56 from NAS Squantum carrier-qualified thirty-three pilots aboard the USS *Franklin D. Roosevelt* (CVA 42). In the process they became the first reserve air group from New England to go to sea. That same year other reservists from various bases carqualed aboard the USS *Cabot*. By the end of the decade, the United States finally had a trained and ready reserve to answer an enemy's threat.

Too late to see service in World War II, the Grumman F8F Bearcat found a home with the Naval Air Reserve, serving in units around the country. These Grummans belong to NAS Denver, one of several naval air stations established after WW II to make drill sites available and accessible to veterans across the country.

POST–WORLD WAR II AIRCRAFT MARKINGS

The reorganization of the Naval Air Reserve following World War II brought with it a new system for marking and identifying reserve aircraft. Starting in 1946, all reserve aircraft carried a 20-inch-wide yellow band placed around the rear fuselage, just ahead of the tail. Other markings that identified the aircraft as belonging to the reserve were the letter *N* in front of or above the aircraft designation number (NF6F-5), or the letter *V* in front of or below the bureau number. Some aircraft carried both of these letters.

Starting in 1947, the twenty-inch color band was expanded to thirty-six inches, and the color was changed to international orange. Also, thirty-six-inch-high identification letters were applied to the vertical tail and to the upper right and lower left wing. Two letters were normally carried, the first indicating the base the aircraft was assigned to and the second reflecting the mission of the aircraft. (Rumor has it that this change in marking was precipitated by the many episodes of "flathat-

Many stalwarts of World War II continued serving the Naval Air Reserve in the late forties, including the F6F Hellcat, once the most common carrier fighter and the leading scorer against the Japanese. The Hellcat was among the first Naval Air Reserve aircraft to be used in carrier requalification after the war. Here, Norfolk-based Hellcats prepare to launch during a CQ.

A Norfolk reserve pilot follows the taxi director up the deck during carrier qualifications. Routine "carquals" by reserve pilots in the late '40s kept them current and proficient. This training paid off during the Korean mobilization.

An SNJ-5 from one of the almost forgotten bases, NAS St. Louis, taxis in 1950. *(Courtesy of Jim Sullivan)*

This early-model Corsair belongs to NRAB Squantum, and is shown outside one of the base hangars in 1948. *(Courtesy of Peter B. Mersky)*

ting"—buzzing and other unauthorized low-level flight maneuvers—that reserve aviators were alleged to have been involved in following the war. The new markings made the aircraft more identifiable, and thus pilots involved in these episodes could be held accountable.)

The lettering code was as follows:

Aircraft Mission

A—Attack	T—Trainer	U—Utility
F—Fighter	P—Patrol	R—Transport

Bases

A—Anacostia	B—Atlanta	C—Columbus
D—Dallas	E—Minnespolis	F—Oakland
G—Livermore	H—Miami	I—Grosse Ile
J—Jacksonville		K—Olathe
L—Akron	L—Los Alamitos	
M—Memphis	N—Spokane	P—Denver
R—New York	S—Norfolk	T—Birmingham
T—Seattle	U—St. Louis	V—Glenview
W—Willow Grove		X—New Orleans
Z—Squantum		

Around 1949, the dual-letter designations were dropped in favor of a single letter identifying the base only.

THE KOREAN WAR

The number, training, and experience of the pilots drilling in the post–World War II reserve paid off dramatically when North Korea invaded South Korea in June 1950. As the conflict grew, it became evident that it would not end quickly. Once again, America geared up for war. The Naval Air Reserve proved to be an invaluable asset in the Korean conflict since the standing forces had been reduced drastically following the end of World War II. Eventually, eighty-four squadrons and 30,000 reservists were called up. Several aviation squadrons volunteered en masse, led by VF-781 at NAS Los Alamitos, California.

The dual-letter marking system was changed to a single letter, designating the base only, in the early fifties. This AD Skyraider is assigned to NAS Gross Ile. (*Courtesy of N. M. Williams*)

41

A Heller HTE-2 lands on the carrier *Philippine Sea* (CV 37). The "Phil Sea" was home to many reservists recalled to active duty for the Korean War.

Naval Air Reserve squadrons contributed a major effort during the Korean War, 1950–53. Some carrier air wings were made up completely of reserve squadrons. This Grumman F9F-2 Panther of VF-831 is on the flight deck of the USS *Antietam* (CVS 36) preparing to launch on a mission against North Korean targets in January 1952.

Reserve aviators also flew AD Skyraiders over Korea. This VA-923 AD is ready to launch from *Bonhomme Richard* in October 1951. *(Courtesy of Jim Sullivan)*

Unfortunately, many of the squadrons were still flying obsolete World War II aircraft and had to transition to newer aircraft such as the AD Skyraider and F9F Panther. Thus, their contributions to the war effort were delayed by the needed retraining, a problem that would continue to plague the reserve in future years. In contrast, those squadrons equipped with F4U Corsairs needed little or no training. They fought gallantly and effectively for both the U.S. Navy and Marine Corps from the start of the war.

The importance of the reserve became more and more apparent as the war dragged on. At one time, the air wing flying off the USS *Bonhomme Richard* (CV 31) consisted entirely of reservists. Reserve squadrons from Olathe, Kansas, Glenview, Illinois, Memphis, Tennessee, and Dallas, Texas, represented 90 percent of the USS *Boxer*'s (CV 21) air wing. At times, air reservists flew 75 percent of all combat sorties. Korea was definitely a "reservist's" war.

Lieutenant Smith: Anonymous Korean War Reservist

The following article was written by Lieutenant Smith, an anonymous reservist who was recalled to active duty during the Korean War. His observations are probably typical of the many pilots and enlisted men who were recalled to fight this "reserve war," and his thoughts give us some insights into what it was like to be a recalled reservist. Years later, the same feelings and emotions expressed in this article were probably felt by reservists mobilized for Berlin, the *Pueblo* crisis, and the Iraqi invasion of Kuwait.

I Flew with CAG-101 My name is Smith. Lieutenant Charles Smith, USNR, to be correct. I'm a naval aviator just back from Korea. Don't want to talk about it? I thank heaven I'm able to talk. But you are right. I don't want to talk about myself, particularly. I want to talk about a lot of guys—ground crewmen, enlisted men, and pilots like myself that I met out there.

I made a promise to those guys. It started out as a joke at first. We had a lot of time on our hands while our carrier, *Boxer,* was en route to Korea. When they found out that I used to be a newspaperman, they would sit around making up corny headlines like "local barber trims commie jet" or "merchant mugs MiG."

Two VF-721 Panthers escort an F9F-2P of VC-61 after a mission in September 1951.

You see, we were all reservists, had civilian jobs, a family maybe. There were shoe salesmen, brokers, garage mechanics and yes, even a barber. Jokingly, I said if I ever got back alive, I'd tell the world their story. As it turned out, their story is no joke. Fred Painter did clobber a YAK that jumped him. Fred owns an appliance shop. Joe Gino, the barber, put the clippers to several air ships before he was through. But let me tell the story from the beginning.

Like I said, we were members of the reserve, the Naval Air Reserve. We used to make weekend trips to the nearest naval air station to maintain our flight proficiency and keep our hands in. Some of us got paid, some didn't. The money didn't matter much.

Sure, we knew we stood a good chance of being called in the event of an emergency or a war. But we got back with the old gang, told sea stories, and had a chance to fly or fool around with planes. Then the training started getting tougher, our flight syllabus kept getting tighter. There was less time for sea stories or coffee after a flight. Toward the end, they were really piling it on us. I guess we all knew it was just a matter of time.

I got my orders in the middle of July. I had just taken the family to the mountains. I had twenty-four hours to report. It was the same with the rest. I found out later that more than 3,100 guys like myself had received similar orders. Twenty-four hours later they were all there. Their businesses, their homes, their families had been left behind. They didn't know where they were going, or exactly what they were going to do. They did know they were ready.

How does a guy feel? What goes through his mind, especially if he has a wife and couple of kids? I remember the tight feeling in my throat

A tractor pulls a VF-721 Panther across *Boxer*'s (CVV 21) flight deck.

and a knot in my stomach. My hands were sweaty, too. I remember saying to myself, "This is it."

Yes, my wife Alice cried a little. She tried hard not to, but women are like that. The kids didn't know what it meant. I could see the question marks in their eyes along with the tears. I knew I'd miss them.

It was harder to go this time, yes a million times harder. Sure, I flew with the Navy in World War II but I was young. The wide blue yonder was a challenge, a challenge to youth. I accepted it eagerly. This time, there was no challenge.

I had no desire to feel a thousand horses pulling me through the air, or the wind clutching my flight jacket. I wanted to laugh and say it was all a big joke. Only it wasn't. Somebody somewhere needed me. I remember I felt like a policeman when I pinned my wings on my greens.

Sure, I could have requested a deferment and probably gotten it; so could the rest of them. But they didn't. Don't ask me why. A man must live with himself, I guess.

But there we were on board USS *Boxer* heading for Korea and God knows what. The intensive training we had received was behind us. It was the first time in naval aviation history that an all-reserve squadron had struck back at the enemy. The eyes of an anxious world were on us.

Some time later we joined *Princeton* and *Valley Forge,* as part of Task Force 77. There were humorous little parodies by the "Happy Valley" boys and bits of verse from the "Sweet Pea." With appropriate ceremony, *Boxer* was dubbed the "Busy Bee." We had joined a great team.

The din of this brief welcome still rang in our ears as we prepared to launch our first aerial attack. No longer "weekend warriors," we were members of Carrier Air Group 101 and part of the Navy, the fighting Navy!

I'm not going to bore you with a long war story. The record of the "Busy Bee" and the Naval Air Reservists that served aboard her speaks for itself. Members of VFI-721, VA-702, VF-791 and VF-884 were in the air more than 20,000 hours and flew over 8,000 sorties against the enemy. Seven thousand enemy casualties resulted. These "butchers, bakers, and candlestick makers" virtually pulverized bridges, railroads and troop concentrations from the 38th parallel to the muddy Yalu.

45

A PBY Catalina, famed for its service in World War II, sits on the ramp at Minneapolis. Throughout the history of the Naval Air Reserve it has been given older aircraft such as this while newer equipment went to the active-duty force. *(Courtesy of Peter B. Mersky)*

Their Corsairs, Skyraiders and Panthers gladdened the hearts of ground troops as they flew in close air support, or their napalm tanks sent seething flame over advance enemy positions. For seven months, these Naval Air Reservists carried the fight to the enemy.

They're home now, or back in the States, just like I am. They left behind them a wonderful record. A record for Naval Air Reservists of *Bonhomme Richard* and *Antietam* to shoot at as they take our place on the team. Perhaps this message from Commander Air Forces, Pacific Fleet will illustrate what I mean:

"The members of the former reserve squadrons of Carrier Air Group 101 have earned the admiration and gratitude of both the Navy and the nation for their magnificent performance of duty while conducting combat operations against the enemy in Korea. Despite losses suffered from the constantly increasing accuracy and intensity of the enemy's antiaircraft fire, you have maintained the aggressiveness that characterized our fighting men, and 7,000 enemy casualties attest to the vigor and determination of your attack. My congratulations to each officer and man for his part in the splendid record the Group has established. Vice Admiral T.L. Sprague."

That's the story of Joe Gino, barber; Fred Painter, merchant; and a host of others just like them. I'm proud to tell the story of these 'modern minutemen.'

There's Alice with the kids. Guess what? We're going to the mountains!

The Norfolk, Virginia, area with its large fleet presence was also a major drawing area for postwar reservists. Here, a squadron of Avenger crewmen conduct a preflight brief beside one of their aircraft.

The Avenger used a dorsal power turret with a single .50-caliber machine gun. These Norfolk reservists conduct familiarization training on one of their squadron's aircraft.

One of the early Lockheed P2V Neptunes, which served the navy in many configurations for almost 40 years and were first assigned to reserve squadrons in the late '40s and early '50s. Here Norfolk reservists arm the patrol bomber's nose-mounted machine guns, which were removed in later models.

An "orphan" of a decelerating development program after World War II, a few of the Martin AM-1 Maulers were assigned to the Naval Air Reserve in the late '40s. These large, powerful attack aircraft were among the last to come from the Martin Company in Baltimore.

One of the largest single-engine aircraft to serve aboard ship, the Grumman AF Guardian also flew, for a brief time, with the Naval Air Reserve. Here, an AF runs up before taxiing at NAS South Weymouth in the mid '50s. Note the powerful searchlight under the port wing. *(Courtesy of Peter B. Mersky)*

POST-KOREA MINUTEMEN

The Naval Air Reserve had more than proved its worth during the Korean War. As hostilities ceased and reservists returned to their civilian jobs, navy planners were concerned that many veterans would not reaffiliate with the reserve, having already fought in two wars and had their lives interrupted by the Korean conflict. To meet this problem, the reserve was divided into different categories of mobilization preparedness. The "ready" reserve could be recalled in an emergency declared by Congress or the president. "Standby" reservists could be recalled only in the event of war or a national emergency declared by Congress. Obviously, the opportunities for active duty and flying were greater for the members of the ready reserve, but there were also flight provisions for standby reservists in drilling units. With their recall eligibility more clearly defined, many World War II and Korean veteran pilots reaffiliated with reserve units, and this pool of priceless experience was maintained.

The Tar Program

Another important administrative change took place early in the fifties with the establishment of the TAR (Training and Administration of Reserves) program. TAR personnel were selected from prior service officers and enlisted. Once designated a TAR, the individual's primary responsibility became training civilian sailors for mobilization readiness. TARs are the backbone and continuity of the reserve training program, and they have played a key role in the aviation reserve over the years.

NAS Minneapolis aircraft of the early 1950s—the FH-1 Phantom, F4U Corsair, and SNJ Texan—fly in formation over the Twin Cities in this unique photograph.

Newer But Not Newest Aircraft for the Fifties

New aircraft started filtering into the reserve force in the fifties as Cougars, Panthers, Skyraiders, and Neptunes phased out Hellcats, Avengers, and Catalinas. Older aircraft were still the rule, however, and not until the sixties would the tactical reserve units complete their transition to jets. The lack of fleet-equivalent aircraft had always been a problem when mobilizations occurred. It was no different in 1961 when yet another world crisis necessitated calling out the reserve forces.

NAS Minneapolis F9F-2 Panthers in the late 1950s. The Panther was one of the first jets flown by Naval Air Reserve squadrons.

The North American FJ-1 Fury was one of the navy's first jet fighters although its success was limited. A few of the tubby little aircraft served with the Naval Air Reserve in the early '50s, including this example from NAS Olathe. Another vintage aircraft is pictured behind the Fury, a Martin P5M "Marlin." *(Courtesy of Peter B. Mersky)*

An R4D from NAS Willow Grove in the late '50s. *(Courtesy of Jim Sullivan)*

50

This 1958 photo shows an R-5D of VR-724 from NAS Glenview over NAS Patuxent River. Transport aircraft of the Naval Air Reserve crossed the country carrying thousands of reservists to weekend drills.

Naval Air Reserve P2Vs operated from coast to coast for well over three decades. It is likely that more reserve airmen saw duty in this aircraft than in any other. This P2V-5 was in service with Oakland squadrons in the 1950s. *(Courtesy of Peter B. Mersky)*

These P2Vs from VP-741 in Jacksonville are flying over the U.S. Naval Base at Guantánamo in 1962. VP-741 and four other VP squadrons were recalled to active duty in response to the Berlin Wall crisis. *(Photo by PHC J.C. Davis)*

The Berlin Wall

In the fall of 1961, East Germany erected the infamous wall dividing East and West Berlin. The wall violated the sixteen-year-old agreement between the wartime Allies to keep Berlin free, and clearly required a response. Calling up the Naval Air Reserve was part of that response.

Thirteen VS (carrier-based antisubmarine) and five VP (patrol/antisubmarine) reserve squadrons were recalled to active duty. Unlike previous mobilizations, these squadrons were not activated to fight a war but to prevent one. The call-up was limited to antisubmarine warfare (ASW) squadrons since the Soviet submarine threat was seen as the greatest danger in the event tensions caused by the wall escalated into conflict. Four thousand reservists and 190 aircraft were involved in the call-up. Squadrons involved in the call-up were as follows:

Squadron	Location
VP-832	NAS New York
VP-933	NAS Willow Grove
VP-741	NARTU Jacksonville
VP-661	NARTU Anacostia
VP-872	NARTU Alameda
VS-837	NAS New York
VS-935	NAS Willow Grove
VS-915	NAS South Weymouth
VS-733	NAS Grosse Ile
VS-821	NAS New Orleans
VS-861	NARTU Norfolk
VS-771	NAS Los Alamitos
VS-772	NAS Los Alamitos
VS-873	NARTU Alameda
VS-891	NAS Seattle
VS-721	NAS Seattle

Thirteen VS (carrier-based antisubmarine) squadrons, flying S-2 Trackers such as these from NARTU Norfolk, were recalled in response to the Berlin crisis. *(Courtesy of Peter B. Mersky)*

Although the Vietnam War did not see as active a participation by Naval Air Reservists as Korea, certain squadrons made important contributions, particularly in the early stages of the U.S. buildup. These C-118s, left and below, from VR-772 made several supply runs from their home base at Los Alamitos, California, to Chu Lai, South Vietnam, in 1966.

An F-6 Skyray taxis at NAS Olathe in May 1964. Prior to 1970 these aircraft were assigned to reserve stations and flown by several squadrons including marine units. *(Photo by Nick Williams)*

The reservists flew ASW patrols in the Caribbean and along the Atlantic Coast as well as barrier patrols along the West Coast. By and large, the reserve forces performed well, and the show of force demonstrated by the mobilization could be considered successful. As in the Korean War, however, the capability to contribute immediately was reduced by the need to transition to new, more-capable and compatible fleet-type aircraft. The P2V-5Fs that the VP squadrons flew were in varying degrees of mechanical condition but not up-to-date by fleet standards in their electronic equipment. The search radar, for example, was so outdated that parts and test support equipment were no longer available in the fleet. Many of the S2Fs were not up-to-date on aircraft service changes, had high-time engines that needed overhaul, and had vital electronic gear used in sub hunting that was out of date. Even with these constraints, however, the reservists were able to achieve operational status and make significant contributions to the navy's ASW capability following their activation. On 1 August 1962, the squadrons were demobilized.

The years following demobilization from the Berlin call-up were quiet for the Naval Air Reserve. The tactical squadrons completed their transition to jets, but again they received "hand-me-downs" from the active-duty navy. While the fleet flew the new F-4 Phantom, late-model F-8 Crusaders, and the A-7 Corsair, reservists were given the F-1 (FJ), A-4Bs and Cs, and the F-8A. Even as the Vietnam War heated up, there was little impetus to upgrade the equipment used by the Naval Air Reserve. Perhaps even more surprising, the reserve role in the Vietnam conflict was limited mostly to cargo and transport efforts. Not until a U.S. intelligence ship, the USS *Pueblo* (AGER 2), was captured in January 1968 would reserve forces be called upon. And then they were called upon in a big way!

Comments of Rear Admiral Frederick Palmer and Vice Admiral P. N. Charbonnet, Former Chiefs of Naval Reserve, Concerning the Nation's Failure to Use More Reserve Forces During the Vietnam War

Rear Admiral Palmer: *"It was a conscious decision in Washington, made by political leaders, including the various presidents and secretaries of defense, that we could have both guns and butter. To mobilize the reserves, they thought, might send the wrong signal. It was not a declared war. Of course, Korea was not a declared war, either, but I was there, and believe me, it was a war!"*

Vice Admiral Charbonnet: *"My association with the Naval Reserve has been long and rewarding. I graduated from the Naval Academy in February 1941 and arrived at my first ship assignment at the same time that reserve mobilization for World War II was commenced. My reserve associates were ROTC graduates, old and new, Naval Cadets who flew our SOCs, and DVGs from Prairie State, Notre Dame, and the Academy. We got along fine, and it really wasn't long before the reservists outnumbered the regulars. World War II was a reserve war, and its successor, Korea, followed the same trend. Although Vietnam had plenty of reservists individually and through select units, the failure of our government to mobilize reserves in a full war footing became a principal failure which was the real disaster of Vietnam."*

THE *PUEBLO* CALL-UP: SUCCESS FROM ADVERSITY

No date has been more important in shaping the role of the Naval Air Reserve today than 23 January 1968. This date, ironically, had nothing to do with the Naval Air Reserve. It was the date when the USS *Pueblo* (AGER 2), an intelligence-gathering ship, was captured by the North Koreans and its crew interned in a North Korean prison. In response to this act of aggression, President Lyndon B. Johnson ordered the immediate recall of six tactical air reserve squadrons to active duty, effective 25 January 1968. As they had done many times before, the reservists "answered the bell," ready and willing to defend their country. Only this time, motivation and patriotism were not enough. The philosophy that reserve forces should fly obsolete, second-generation aircraft had degraded reserve readiness throughout the history of the reserve flying program. Only in the *Pueblo* call-up, however, did the fallacy of

USS *Pueblo,* (AGER 2) as it appeared shortly before its capture by North Korea in January 1968.

This Los Alamitos A-4B from VA-776 carries an in-flight refueling store on the centerline station. VA-776 was one of six TACAIR squadrons mobilized as a result of the *Pueblo* crisis.

this philosophy become apparent. Despite the hard work, dedication, and sacrifices of many recalled reservists, the squadrons were unable to achieve the level of readiness expected of them. Eight months after the recall, the squadrons were released from active duty.

Many valuable lessons were learned from this mobilization. As a result, the entire Naval Air Reserve organization was restructured to address and remedy the problems faced by the mobilized squadrons. Had it not been for the *Pueblo* call-up, the air reserve may never have reached the state of preparedness and capability it enjoys today. To understand why this is so, it is necessary to study the problems that existed during the call-up.

Six tactical air (TACAIR) squadrons were mobilized: three fighter (VF) and three attack (VA). The fighter squadrons, flying F-8As and Bs, were VF-661, NAF Washington, D.C., VF-703, NAS Dallas, Texas, and VF-931, NAS Willow Grove, Pennsylvania. The attack squadrons, flying A-4Bs, were VA-776, NAS Los Alamitos, California, VA-873, NAS Alameda, California, and VA-831, NAS New York. These squadrons were selected for mobilization based on chief of naval reserve training's evaluations of the most ready TACAIR squadrons in the reserve.

The chief of naval operations (CNO) issued the mobilization orders on the afternoon of 25 January 1968, with a reporting date for all mem-

VA-776 eventually relocated from NAS Los Alamitos to NAS Alameda where it would be based during the mobilization call-up. Here Commander Milton E. Johnson, squadron CO, taxis in after a training flight on 30 January 1968, just five days after the recall order was issued. The squadron later exchanged its "Bravos" for A-4Fs. *(Photo by JOSN J. W. Fletcher)*

bers of midnight, 26 January 1968. With few exceptions, reservists answered the short-notice recall promptly, expecting to be on their way to Korea. In reality, however, President Johnson initiated the call-up more as a show of force than as a planned action to augment the fleet to retaliate against the Koreans.

With no specific tasking for the reserve, the decision was made to rotate the reserve squadrons into an active-duty deployment cycle. Three squadrons would deploy to the Med and three to WestPac. Prior to these deployments, the squadrons would move from their reserve bases and train at active-duty bases (Naval Air Stations Cecil Field, Miramar, and Alameda).

Problems arose almost immediately. Reservists were flying obsolete aircraft, handed down from the fleet when it acquired new equipment. The fighter squadrons' F-8s were not carrier suitable without three nose-gear modifications. Also, these early-model Crusaders had only a manual fire-control system that limited the aircraft to daylight visual weather conditions. The A-4Bs flown by the attack squadrons were even further away from combat readiness. These Skyhawks required at least nine major aircraft service changes to be considered combat ready. Included in these changes were important items such as armor plating, multiple bomb ejector rack capability, and electronic countermeasures equipment.

Since the chief of naval air reserve training did not have aircraft suitable for deployment, combat-ready airplanes had to be transferred from active-duty inventories, already stretched thin by the Vietnam War. These transfers could not be effected immediately, so the reservists were forced to train initially in their old aircraft, and then start new training cycles as they received the more modern, advanced, and capable fleet aircraft such as the F-8H and A-4E.

Early Model F-8s, like those assigned to NAS Willow Grove flown by VF-931, were not carrier-suitable. This was a major problem during the *Pueblo* call-up, because the pilots were not carrier-qualified and could not "bounce" on the field to practice until later model F-8s were transferred to them.

Prior to the *Pueblo* crisis, reserve aircraft were assigned to air stations, not squadrons, and flown by both the navy and marines. The weaknesses in this system became apparent when VF-661 was mobilized, leaving the marine units with no aircraft to fly once the squadron left for Cecil Field. This Crusader was shared by navy and marine pilots at NAF Washington, D.C.

Training was further hampered by poor aircraft availability. The lack of flyable aircraft was a central problem throughout the call-up. There were several reasons for this. Parts support was poor for the older aircraft, and they were given a lower supply priority than the fleet during initial stages of the call-up. More significantly, there were just not enough trained, experienced, and capable enlisted people to fix the aircraft and supervise the maintenance program. Most of the heavy-duty "real" maintenance at the squadrons' home bases had been done by the full-time active-duty TARs. Those TAR mechanics were attached to the naval air station that owned the aircraft and were not part of the mobilizing squadrons. When the reserve units detached from their home base without the TARs, the lack of maintenance expertise showed up sorely. Also, many of the reserve petty officers—those who should have been the supervisors—simply did not have the technical knowledge or background that their grade indicated. As one second-class petty officer put it, "Although I had been with the squadron for four years and made three cruises [two-week periods of annual duty for training], I had never de-armed and removed an ejection seat, never worked on a canopy and never trouble-shot an air-conditioning and pressurization system."

The squadrons also had trouble acquiring basic tools, publications, instructions, and know-how in current maintenance procedures. In a post-mobilization report, one squadron maintenance officer reported, "There was a total lack of supplies, active-duty forms and labor-saving devices. Hand and power tools were not available until two and one-half months after mobilization, and a portion of IMRL gear was never received. Technical pubs were not immediately available. Material Control and Maintenance Administration were two critical areas where we had little expertise. Maintenance men had not been trained in 3M and current maintenance practices."

Compounding the maintenance problems was a steady stream of aircraft transfers. The active-duty navy, struggling to find combat-ready aircraft for the reserve squadrons from its own inventory, was forced to juggle aircraft to meet the most immediate priority. One group of aircraft would be transferred so that the reserve squadrons could start their training cycle, and then later, another group of combat-ready and deployable aircraft would be assigned. The result was an inordinate number of aircraft transfers that added significantly to the reserve squadrons' maintenance load.

There was also a problem with pilot qualifications and currency. The overall experience level of the squadrons looked good at first glance, but closer scrutiny revealed that many of the pilots lacked time in model and carrier-landing experience in jet aircraft. VF-931, for example, was scheduled to deploy with F-8s, arguably the most difficult aircraft in the navy to land on a carrier. Of sixteen assigned pilots, five had never made a carrier landing in the F-8, including the commanding officer and executive officer (XO). The XO had a total of six carrier landings, none in jets. Two more pilots had never made a night F-8 carrier landing. Dallas-based VF-703 pilots averaged 180 carrier landings, but three pilots had no carrier landings at all, let alone in the F-8. VA-776 had three pilots without any carrier landings, and VA-831 had one.

To complicate the situation further, some of the most experienced pilots in the squadrons had already logged two combat tours in Vietnam and thus were restricted from deploying to WestPac. Finally, two of the F-8 squadrons, VF-661 and VF-931, were scheduled to deploy aboard the USS *Shangri-La* (CVA 38). The *Shangri-La* was one of several older, *Essex*-class carriers (designated 27C) that had the smallest decks of any carrier in the navy. In VF-931's post-mobilization summary, the aviation safety officer summed up the situation as follows: "One can only throw up one's arms in disbelief at a reserve squadron flying F-8s aboard a 27C-class carrier at night, in winter, with a pitching deck. Experienced aviators shudder at the thought, much less week-end warriors . . . "

Despite the many adversities, the reservists pressed on and trained to the best of their ability. As the mobilization wore on, the reserve squadrons started to heal. Parts priority was upgraded to the same level as that of the fleet. Additional reservists filled out the squadron's complement. TARs were assigned from air stations to furnish maintenance and administrative expertise, and the squadrons became accustomed to active-duty paperwork, the supply system, and fleet operations. Twenty pilots from VA-873 completed day and night carrier qualifications, as did pilots from VF-703. Nevertheless, eight months after the mobilization, the squadrons had completed less than 75 percent of their training syllabus. VA-873 reported a completion of only 59 percent. A scheduled work-up cruise aboard the USS *Ranger* (CVA 61) the following month was canceled and VA-155, an active-duty attack squadron, was inserted in the reserve squadron's place. VF-931 reported 50 percent of its flight syllabus complete with no pilots qualified in carrier landings or air-to-air operations.

On 16 September 1968, the CNO issued a message releasing the six reserve squadrons. The reasons given for the deactivation were the reduced military posture in the Korean area and budget cuts totaling almost three billion dollars for FY 69. These cuts led to an early release program for certain active-duty personnel, and the navy felt that it couldn't justify keeping the recalled reservists on active-duty given these early outs. How big a factor the reserve's readiness situation played in the decision is difficult to determine. Although the squadrons did not meet original or revised deployment schedules, the progress they had made indicated that they could have deployed, with a somewhat limited

Washington-based VF-661 transferred to NAS Cecil Field where it planned to exchanged its F-8Bs for "Hotels" during the *Pueblo* call-up. Shortages of combat-ready F-8s led to long delays in aircraft delivery, however, and the squadron had been mobilized for over seven months before it received the first of its F-8Hs. Ironically, the squadron was demobilized shortly after receiving its new aircraft. This photo, showing the new Crusaders in their Air Wing Eight colors, was taken the day before the squadron's flight funding was terminated.

combat capability, sometime in 1969 if required. But whatever the reason, the release of reservists in the fall of 1968 was clearly the prudent course of action.

In retrospect, the problems surrounding the *Pueblo* mobilization could be attributed more to the prevailing philosophy of a reserve force than to a lack of performance by the Naval Air Reserve and the reservists who were called up. In reality, many experienced, motivated, and dedicated people proved they were willing to make many personal and business sacrifices to "answer the bell" when called. The preponderance of recalled reservists accepted the call-up as part of their reserve responsibility and worked long and hard to achieve combat readiness despite the many obstacles they encountered. No, the real "villain" in the *Pueblo* fiasco was not the people of the Naval Air Reserve but rather the institutional neglect that had plagued the air reserve force almost from its beginning. Defense planners and Congress wanted a reserve force that was immediately deployable, but they were not willing to equip it with modern equipment or fund it adequately to ensure its people had training appropriate to their mission. Virtually identical problems had plagued every mobilization, but only in the spotlight of a short-notice, high-visibility call-up did these deficiencies become obvious.

The *Pueblo* mobilization was a critically important event in the history of the Naval Air Reserve because it focused attention on the factors necessary to have a truly ready reserve. Even as the six squadrons were demobilizing, top navy officers were analyzing the call-up in an attempt to build a better reserve. They determined that the following problems were the most significant:

• The Naval Air Reserve was assigned obsolescent aircraft that were not combat ready, were difficult to maintain and support, and were not compatible with fleet ships and air wings.
• Enlisted personnel with suitable background and training to support a full mobilization were not assigned in sufficient numbers.
• Reserve squadrons operated away from the fleet and were not familiar with current procedures.
• Reserve training was not realistic and up-to-date, constrained in many cases by airspace problems and a lack of modern equipment.

• Sufficient funding had to be provided to allow reserve aviators enough flight time to maintain their necessary qualifications.

With the problems of the *Pueblo* call-up clearly identified, the navy could move ahead to create a reserve that was truly ready. On 1 April 1970, two reserve carrier air wings were established (CVWRs 20 and 30). This was the first step of a plan to modernize the reserve forces and reorganize them in a manner that mirrored the active-duty forces. The new era of the Naval Air Reserve began on this day and signaled the beginning of two decades of dramatic improvements in funding, equipment, readiness, and capability. Many mistakes were made that led to the fiasco during the *Pueblo* call-up. Fortunately, the nation learned from these mistakes and took the necessary action that has led to the unprecedented success enjoyed by the Naval Air Reserve today.

Comments of Vice Admiral P. N. Charbonnet Concerning the *Pueblo* Mobilization:

"One of my most pleasant reflections during my career was my constant association with reservists on active duty and during their yearly training on ships in which I served. Large numbers extended their active duty into productive careers from which our navy greatly benefited.

"I was also involved with failures in the reserve's performance. Without fail, the basic causes were the result of mismanagement by the regular navy, a lack of mutual understanding before the call-up, and unrealistic training with inadequate equipment."

The *Pueblo* mobilization focused on TACAIR squadrons, but problems uncovered during the call-up were common to all communities in the Naval Air Reserve. The P-2 Neptune served the navy well for over thirty years, but it was another example of a reserve aircraft that had become outmoded in the '60s and ill-equipped for the ASW mission by the end of the decade. This aircraft was assigned to NAS Los Alamitos.

REORGANIZATION

Without a doubt, the *Pueblo* call-up had hurt the reputation of the Naval Air Reserve and raised questions about its effectiveness and worth. Something needed to be done about reserve readiness—and done right away—lest the whole concept of a ready reserve be jeopardized. And something *was* done right away. Even as the squadrons were demobilizing, the navy was conducting intensive evaluations of the problems experienced during the call-up. The navy realized that it had to make some major modifications to the reserve program before the Naval Air Reserve could be the truly ready organization that the nation's defense demanded. Those major modifications were soon made.

Within a year, the Naval Air Reserve was totally reorganized to mirror the structure of the active-duty forces. As Rear Admiral H. E. Greer, Chief of Naval Air Reserve Training at the time put it,

"We are going to reorganize to duplicate the fleet; the reserve squadron structure is going to be identical to the fleet squadron. Our squadrons are going to be the same in manpower, in numbers of aircraft assigned, in maintenance procedures, in reporting procedures and in funding."

This reorganization plan became the springboard that enabled today's reserve to reach unprecedented levels of readiness. The plan established

After the 1970 reorganization, the reserve VA squadrons received updated Skyhawks, including A-4Ls, remanufactured A-4Cs with upgraded avionics. This "Lima" from VA-205 is shown during initial carrier qualifications aboard the USS *John F. Kennedy* (CV 67) in August 1971. *(Photo by PH1 Paul L. Schlappich)*

two reserve tactical carrier air wings (CVWR), two reserve antisubmarine air groups (CVSGR), twelve patrol (VP) squadrons, and four transport (VR) units. Commanding officers of the reserve force squadrons assumed custody and responsibility for their own aircraft and reported directly to their wing commander, an active-duty officer. Additionally, squadrons were manned with enough TAR officers and enlisted men to form a cadre of trained personnel that could maintain operational continuity. Naval air reservists filled out the remainder of the squadrons. These reservists, particularly the aviators, were carefully screened for background and qualifications, and were funded for increased participation, including carrier qualifications if applicable. Where feasible, units were relocated to active-duty bases where they could take advantage of fleet facilities, work more closely with the active-duty forces, and be in position in the event of mobilization.

The Naval Air Reserve formed a flight demonstration team, "The Air Barons," in 1969 from VA-209 at NAS Glenview. Flying A-4Bs and later A-4Ls, the team operated until 1972. VA-209 was initially assigned to CVWR-20 in lieu of a fighter squadron.

Tactical Reserve Air Wings

CVWR-20 and -30 were established on 1 April 1970. These air wings were organized with a mix of squadrons typical of a tactical fleet air wing assigned to an *Essex*-class aircraft carrier. The air wings were organized as shown in table 1.

Due to a shortage of combat-capable fighter aircraft, CVWR-20 was initially assigned five attack squadrons. VA-209 and VA-210 were disestablished in the summer of 1971, replaced by VF-201 and VF-202, flying F-8Hs out of NAS Dallas, Texas. VF-201 and -202 were reassigned from CVWR-30 to CVWR-20, while VF-301 and -302, flying F-8Js, were established at NAS Miramar. With two fighter squadrons assigned to each air wing, the new reserve air wings were able to perform all the missions of their active-duty counterparts.

The reorganization also included upgrading the aircraft assigned to the reserve. F-8As and -Bs gave way to F-8H, -J, -K and -L models for the fighter squadrons. Reserve attack squadrons started flying A-4Cs and

Table 1. Organization of Air Wings

Squadron	Aircraft	Location
CVWR-30		
VA-303	A-4C	NAS Alameda, CA
VA-304	A-4C	NAS Alameda, CA
VAQ-308	EKA-3B	NAS Alameda, CA
VF-201	F-8H	NAS Dallas, TX
VF-202	F-8H	NAS Dallas, TX
VA-305	A-4C	NAS Point Mugu, CA
VFP-306	RF-8G	NAF Washington, DC
VAW-307	E-1B	NAS North Island, CA
CVWR-20		
VA-203	A-4L	NAS Jacksonville, FL
VA-204	A-4L	NAS Memphis, TN
VA-205	A-4L	NAS Atlanta, GA
VA-209	A-4L	NAS Glenview, IL
VA-210	A-4B/C	NAS South Weymouth, MA
VAW-207	E-1B	NAS Norfolk, VA
VFP-206	RF-8G	NAF Washington, DC
VAQ-208	EKA-3B	NAS Alameda, CA

A-4Ls instead of A-4Bs. E-1Bs and EKA-3B and RF-8G photo-reconnaissance aircraft rounded out the air wing. These aircraft were, for the most part, one generation removed from the equipment the fleet was flying, but they nevertheless represented a first step in upgrading the hardware flown by the reserve squadrons.

The first test for the newly reorganized tactical reserve air wings was carrier qualifications. No single factor hurt the *Pueblo* squadrons' mobilization readiness more than their lack of carrier currency. Clearly, if the Naval Air Reserve was going to be a viable and ready force, their aircraft and pilots had to be qualified to deploy aboard ship. Starting in the fall of 1970, CVWR-20 and -30 conducted carrier qualifications (carquals) aboard three different carriers. By 23 November, eighty pilots from CVWR-20 and sixty seven from CVWR-30 carrier-qualified without incident. The newly organized reserve had passed its first test with flying colors.

The next logical test was to see if the entire air wing could mobilize and operate off a carrier. The answer was a resounding yes. CVWR-20 embarked aboard the *John F. Kennedy* (CVA 67) in August 1971 for two weeks of active-duty training. The squadrons operated as an embarked air wing, and underwent an operational readiness inspection (ORI). Air Wing 20 received an overall grade of "Excellent." The reputation of the new Naval Air Reserve was on the rise.

The revamping of the reserve force also resulted in a major administrative change for the Office of the Chief of Naval Air Reserve. On 1 February 1973, the two large components of the Naval Reserve—air and surface—were consolidated into a single command: the Chief of Naval Reserve. Prior to the consolidation, the surface reserve force had been administered from facilities in Omaha, Nebraska—the reasoning being that this site was approximately in the middle of the country—

As part of the reorganization, four reserve fighter squadrons and two light photoreconnaissance squadrons received upgraded models of the Vought Crusader. VF-301 eventually operated F-8Js. One of the Devil's Disciples' "Juliets" is readied for a launch from the *Roosevelt* (CV 42), while a VFP-306 RF-8G is waved off overhead. (*Courtesy Peter B. Mersky*)

while the Naval Air Reserve had its headquarters at NAS Glenview, Illinois. New Orleans was chosen as the location for the new command.

As the reserve continued its outstanding performance, the concept of the "total-force navy"—active and reserve forces working together and sharing missions for the common defense—gained more credibility and support. Newer aircraft entered the reserve wings. In 1974 the attack squadrons moved from Skyhawks into A-7As, and VF-301 and -302 transitioned to F-4Bs. (VF-22L1 at NAS Los Alamitos was actually the first reserve F-4 squadron, but it was in operation only from January 1969 to October 1970.) The E-1B Trackers gave way to E-2B Hawkeyes assigned

KA-3Bs gave the new reserve air wings aerial refueling capability. VAK-208 and VAK-308 "Whales" also operated regularly with fleet units, providing tanker services and pathfinder navigation for overwater ferry flights. This 308 Skywarrior was photographed near Northern California's Mt. Shasta.

A reserve pilot from VFP-206, NAF Washington, snags an arresting cable during the squadron's first carrier-qualification period in 1971 aboard the USS *Roosevelt*. TACAIR pilots attached to squadrons that deploy aboard aircraft carriers maintain proficiency by frequent trips to the "boat."

Reserve squadrons continued to improve as they received newer aircraft such as the A-7A flown by VA-304. CVWR attack squadrons won the first bombing derby they entered, competing against active-duty squadrons.

to VAW-78 and -88 in late 1976 to early 1977. With the newer aircraft came increased capability. The reserve was headed in the right direction.

The Naval Air Reserve Tactical Air Wing Test

Reservist proficiency and capability continued to improve as the seventies progressed. The wind-down of the Vietnam War made available many well-qualified and experienced aviators, meaning the reserve squadrons could be highly selective. The result was a buildup of talent and experience that paid big dividends. Reserve Carrier Air Wing Thirty attack squadrons, flying their newly acquired A-7As, finished first, second, and fourth in the annual West Coast bombing derby, competing against active-duty forces. CVWR-20 completed an Operational Readiness Evaluation (ORE) that tested their skill against the same standards used by their active-duty counterparts. The overall grade of the ORE was "Outstanding." Vice Admiral Houser, deputy chief of naval operations for air warfare at the time, stated:

"It is obvious that CVWR-20 is performing commensurate with the highest of fleet standards. This is as it should be, for implicit with the Total Force policy as emphasized by the Congress and Secretary of Defense, is the fact that the Reserve Forces will be used as the initial and primary augmentation of the active forces. You have set an example to emulate." Clearly, the Naval Air Reserve was erasing the doubts of the

Early F-4Bs were traded for F-4Ns—remanufactured "Bravos"—in the late 1970s. *(Courtesy Peter B. Mersky)*

An A-7A of VA-305 over the USS *Ranger* (CV 61) during the initial carrier-qualification phase of the TACAIR test in November of 1976. The TACAIR test ·was an in-depth evaluation of the re-organized reserve wing's readiness and mobilization capability. *(Photo by Eliot Tozer)*

A KA-3B of VAQ-308 recovers aboard USS *Ranger* (CV 61) during the CQ phase of the two-week cruise in November 1976. *(Photo by Peter B. Mersky)*

The morning of the last launch during the TACAIR test. As a final exercise, forty aircraft were launched on an alpha strike against "enemy" forces. The success of this launch and the TACAIR test in general validated the readiness of the Naval Air Reserve and assured their role in the future. *(Photo by Peter B. Mersky)*

Pueblo era and establishing a reputation for professionalism and capability that transcended active-duty/reserve lines. The old days of "Weekend Warriors" and "The Navy Flying Club" were fast disappearing.

Rear Admiral J. D. Ramage, Chief of Naval Air Reserve 1972-74, Comments on the Naval Air Reserve Reorganization:

"Capt. Joe Tully commanded Fleet Air Lemoore, which later became Light Attack Wing, Pacific. In the Spring of 1973, he was holding a bombing derby for the regular squadrons at Lemoore. I asked him if I could enter VA-303 and VA-304. My guys all had at least two tours in Vietnam. As you might guess, the reserves won every competition. Tully said I had sandbagged him. True!"

Old memories die hard, however. As good as the Naval Air Reserve had become after the reorganization, lingering doubts remained whether the new air wings could pack up, deploy aboard an aircraft carrier, conduct cyclic ops, and "project power" immediately after a recall. To see if the new CVWR squadrons could "hack it," Congress mandated a Naval Air Reserve tactical air test. The TACAIR test was scheduled for November 1976 aboard the USS *Ranger* (CV 61). All CVWR-30 squadrons would report aboard the *Ranger* for two weeks of active duty for training. Squadrons would fly day and night cyclic operations, just

Maintenance personnel put in long hours aboard ship keeping their aircraft mission-ready. Here, a group of VF-302 mechs inspect one of their Phantom's in-flight refueling probe. *(Courtesy of Peter B. Mersky)*

like an embarked active-duty air wing, and would be given an operational readiness evaluation during the two weeks. This would be the ultimate test—with the future of the Naval Air Reserve and the "total-force" concept on the line.

On 6 November 1976, the eight squadrons of CVWR-30 embarked in the USS *Ranger*. In the following two weeks, the air wing flew over 1,100 sorties, logging more than 2,200 flight hours and 1,048 carrier landings. Three hundred sixty-five of those arrested landings were at night. The TACAIR test was an unqualified success. The overall ORE score was "Outstanding," and CVWR-30 proved to all doubters that reserve squadrons were ready and able to provide immediate support for the nation's defense when called upon. Vice Admiral Charbonnet, chief of Naval Air

Steam rises from a previous launch as crewmen position an RF-8G from VFP-306 on the No. 4 waist catapult. Note the characteristic raised wing of the F-8 series. Reservists conducted day and night cyclic operations during the TACAIR test.

Reserve, summarized the air wing's accomplishments in a message he sent to them following the exercise:

"The outstanding performance of Carrier Air Wing 30 in the recent ORE aboard USS Ranger is noted with great pleasure. From my personal observation it is clearly apparent that Air Wing 30 can match its record, its combat readiness and elan with any and all fleet carrier air wings."

Similar accolades came from the active-duty forces. Vice Admiral Coogan, commander, Naval Air Forces Pacific sent a message saying, in part, "The success of CVWR-30 during your ORE on Ranger serves as an example for all." Rear Admiral Paul Speer, commander, Carrier Group One sent the following message to CVWR-30:

"Your outstanding planning, scheduling, support and execution of the Reserve Airwing Test were superb. The professional, enthusiastic teamwork between USS Ranger and CVWR-30 by each sailor and officer was a pleasurable experience to behold. Well done."

Turboprop E-2Bs like the one pictured from VAW-78 gave the reserve airwings greatly increased capability in airborne early-warning radar detection.

The success of the TACAIR test was not achieved without cost. Commander Mike Plattis, executive officer of VA-305, was killed in an operational accident during night operations. Sacrifices for the national defense are nothing new for the Naval Air Reserve, however. Fortunately, the tragedy of Commander Plattis's death did not obscure the dramatic success of the TACAIR test, and the Naval Air Reserve was able to continue its steady progress toward more capability and readiness.

Former Chief of Naval Air Reserve Vice Admiral Charbonnet/Comments on the TACAIR Test:

"Shortly after I took over as chief of Naval Air Reserve we deployed a reserve tactical air wing aboard ship in what became known as the TACAIR test. There was some doubt in Congress and among senior defense officials that the reserve squadrons would be able to perform. We recognized the possibility—even probability—that a "failure" might be used as evidence in a case to wrest aircraft from the Naval Air Reserve. Fortunately, the TACAIR test was a resounding success that proved the TACAIR capability of the Naval Air Reserve. I've never seen any air group or wing more capable of taking a flight or any kind of mission at any time than those pilots and crews. Of course, almost every one of them had a hundred missions up the Red River [Vietnam]. I remember that Admiral Speer, the carrier division commander, was both surprised and impressed by these aircrews, and had nothing but praise for them."

New Aircraft for the 1980s

The late seventies saw continued improvement in the aircraft of the reserve squadrons. Attack squadrons transitioned to the A-7B, the VAW squadrons received E-2B Hawkeye early-warning aircraft, and the VAQ squadrons received updated and newer KA-3B aircraft along with a designation change to VAK to reflect their primary mission—aerial refueling. Also, the reserve air wings attained a new electronic-countermeasures

All twelve squadron aircraft pose for a unique photo over the Texas landscape. This photo of VF-202's F-4Ns represents an accomplishment that is a tribute to the mechanics and ground crews who provided the "up" and ready airplanes of the entire squadron. *(Courtesy of Peter B. Mersky)*

VAQ squadrons were redesignated VAK in the late '70s to reflect their primary mission—aerial refueling.

The 1970 reorganization created two reserve ASW carrier air groups. The S-2E from VS-82, NARTU Alameda, was assigned to CVSGR-80. *(Photo by R. E. Kling)*

This E-1B from VAW-88, NAS North Island, was initially assigned to CVSGR-80. When the wing was disestablished in 1976, VAW-88 came under the control of CVWR-30. *(Photo by R. E. Kling)*

capability with the establishment of EA-6A squadrons VAQ-209 at NAS Norfolk and VAQ-309 at NAS Whidbey Island.

The Reserve ASW Carrier Air Groups

The TACAIR squadrons and air wings were the most visible units in the reorganized reserve, but they were by no means the only air reserve squadrons that distinguished themselves. The 1970 reorganization plan for the reserve called for two reserve carrier air groups in addition to the two tactical carrier air wings. The two carrier air groups, composed primarily of carrier-based antisubmarine squadrons, were designated CVSGR-70 and CVSGR-80, and were home-ported at NAS Norfolk and NAS North Island, respectively. The squadrons making up these air groups are shown in table 2.

The CVSGR squadrons shared the same goals as their CVWR counterparts: align with the fleet and train to reach the highest readiness capability possible. Toward this goal, all the fixed-wing squadrons carrier-qualified aboard the USS *Franklin D. Roosevelt* (CV 42) shortly after their establishment and regularly conducted shipboard operations during subsequent active-duty training sessions. CVSGR-80 established a first in 1972 when it embarked the entire air wing aboard the USS *Ticonderoga* (CVS 14) for two weeks of cyclic, antisubmarine-warfare operations. Like its TACAIR counterparts aboard the *Ranger*, CVSGR squadrons showed their capability and earned the respect of the active-duty forces. Captain Edward Boyd, commanding officer of the *Ticonderoga*, sent the following message to the officers and men of CVSGR-80 following their two weeks of active duty:

"During your two weeks of training I gained an even greater appreciation of the potential of our nation's Naval Air Reserve Force. After observing ASW and launch and landing operations, I can assure you that CVSGR-80 is a reserve group ready to be recalled for active service and merge into the tempo of ASW operations without any break in step. It is gratifying to hold this conviction."

In 1976, CVSGR-70 and -80 were disestablished. The capability of the CVSGR officers and men was never in question, but the aircraft they were flying were obsolete and the ASW aircraft carriers they were designed to deploy on had been phased out of the active-duty forces. Unlike the "old days," when the reserve forces may have continued to operate without a real mobilization potential, the reorganized reserve instead looked for a better way to employ its officers and men. The two fixed-wing early-warning squadrons (VAW-78 and -88) were assigned to the operational control of CVWR-20 and -30; the A-4 VSF and the S-2E squadrons were disestablished, and the helicopter squadrons were reorganized under Commander Helicopter Wing Reserve (COMHELWINGRES).

Table 2. Squadrons of CVSGR-70/-80

Squadron	Home Base	Aircraft
VS-71/VS-81	NAS Lakehurst, NJ/NAS Los Alamitos, CA	S-2E
VS-72/VS-82	NAS Norfolk, VA/NARTU Alameda, CA	S 2E
VS-73/VS-83	NAS Lakehurst, NJ/NARTU Whidbey, WA	S-2E
HS-75/HS-84	NAS Lakehurst, NJ/NAS Los Alamitos, CA	SH3A
VAW-78/88	NAS Norfolk, VA/NARTU North Island, CA	E-1B
VSF-76/VSF-86	NAS New Orleans, LA	A-4C
HS-74/HS-85	NAS Quonset Point, RI/NARTU Alameda, CA	SH3A

Reserve Helicopter Reorganization

With the establishment of COMHELWINGRES, all reserve rotary-wing squadrons, east and west coasts, were consolidated under one command. The SH-3 squadrons from CVSGR-70 and -80 were put under the new wing's control, along with some other units that would give the reserves new capability in rotary-wing operations. A new helicopter squadron, HC-9, was established in August 1975 and transferred to the control of COMHELWINGRES in 1976. Flying eight Sikorsky HH-3A "Big Mother" helicopters, HC-9 was the reserve's first squadron with a primary mission of overland combat search and rescue. It also represented the entire navy's *only* squadron with this mission. The significance of this was clear: the "One Navy" concept was gaining acceptance and momentum.

This HH-3A "Big Mother" was assigned to HC-9, the Naval Air Reserve's first and only squadron dedicated to combat SAR (search and rescue).

Helicopter ASW (HS) reserve squadrons received H-3 Sea Kings after the 1970 reorganization. Here an H-3 from HS-74 stands on the South Weymouth ramp in 1976. In that year all reserve rotary-wing aircraft were consolidated under the control of Commander Helicopter Wing Reserve. *(Photo by PH3 T. Cochran)*

Two reserve helicopter gunship squadrons, HAL-4, NAS Norfolk, and HAL-5, NAS Pt. Mugu, carried on the mission of HAL-3, the navy's Seawolf squadron of Vietnam fame. Many decorated, combat-experienced helicopter pilots who left active duty in the '70s joined Naval Air Reserve helicopter squadrons, thus retaining a wealth of talent in the total-force navy. This HH-1K is from HAL-5.

HC-9 maintained its role as the navy's only combat SAR squadron until it was disestablished in 1990.

Also coming under the COMHELWINGRES fold about a year later was another first of its kind for the Naval Air Reserve: the helicopter gunship. HAL-4, flying HH-1Ks, was established in July 1976 at Norfolk, Virginia. The role of HAL-4 was to support Naval Special Warfare Group 2 and other navy units with quick reaction, close air support similar to that provided by the UH-1B Huey gunships of HAL-3 in Vietnam. A second HAL squadron, HAL-5, was established the following year at NAS Pt. Mugu, California.

Patrol Squadrons

The reorganization included the establishment of twelve land-based antisubmarine patrol (VP) squadrons. At the time of the reorganization, the patrol squadrons flew mostly SP-2H Neptunes, although three squadrons—VP-62, VP-91, and VP-68—had the newer, more capable P-3A

Orion. The squadrons were located as follows:

VP-60 and VP-90	NAS Glenview, IL
VP-62	NAS Jacksonville, FL
VP-64 and 66	NAS Willow Grove, PA
VP-68	NAS Patuxent River, MD
VP-92	NAS South Weymouth, MA
VP-94	NAS New Orleans, LA
VP-65	NAS Pt. Mugu, CA
VP-67	NAS Memphis, TN
VP-69	NAS Whidbey Island, WA
VP-91	NAS Moffett Field, CA

*VP-93 was established at NAF Detroit in 1976.

Initially, the four westernmost VP squadrons (VP-65, -67, -69, -91) were assigned under the Commander, Fleet Air Reserve Wing Pacific at NAS Moffett. This command was redesignated Commander, Reserve Patrol Wing Pacific in July 1973, and VP-60 and -90 at NAS Glenview were assigned to their control.

On 1 July 1976, the remaining VP squadrons were put under the

VP-66, one of two patrol squadrons based at NAS Willow Grove, operated the SP-2H until 1973 when it transitioned to the P-3A.

This P-2H Neptune from VP-92, assigned to NAS South Weymouth, was one of twelve land-based ASW patrol squadrons established as part of the reorganization.

A VP-91 P-3A from NAS Moffett Field, is pictured over the Golden Gate Bridge with San Francisco in the distance. VP-91 was one of the first patrol squadrons to receive the "Orions" immediately after the 1970 reorganization.

VP-65 P-3A in company with a P-3C from VP-40, a fleet squadron, demonstrates the "total-force" concept, a phrase used frequently to describe integration of reserve components into the mission of the navy. Reserve VP squadrons have repeatedly demonstrated their ability to meet operational commitments. The integration of reserve forces into the Maritime Patrol community is one of the real success stories of the Naval Air Reserve over the last two decades.

control of Commander, Reserve Patrol Wing Atlantic (COMRESPATWING-LANT) at NAS Norfolk. By this time, all patrol squadrons, both east and west coast, had completed transition to the P-3A Orion and were ready to assume a major role in the navy's antisubmarine mission.

The VP mission proved to be ideally suited for reserve participation. With modern (even if not the most modern) aircraft and highly experienced crews, the reservists could make significant contributions to the navy's overall ASW capability, while at the same time maintaining their own proficiency. This fact was not lost on the active-duty P-3 squadrons. Initially, reserve P-3 crews on active duty for training augmented fleet squadrons on deployments and flew missions side by side with the active-duty squadrons. In 1979, however, reserve squadrons scored a first when VP-60 and VP-90 replaced regular navy P-3 squadrons at NAF Lajes, Azores, and assumed their ASW commitment. On the West Coast, VP-91 deployed to Adak, Alaska, for two months, relieving the active-duty squadrons deployed there. Since then, reserve squadrons have steadily increased their share of the ASW load and now regularly train at active-duty sites at Kadena, Japan, NAS Bermuda, NS Rota, Spain, NAF Lajes, Azores, and Sigonella, Sicily, to assume ASW missions. Today, it would be safe to say that the navy simply could not meet its ASW responsibilities were it not for the participation of the Naval Air Reserve. Additionally, P-3 reserve crews have become increasingly active in drug-interdiction programs and regularly participate in fleet exercises, augmenting active-duty squadrons in these missions. This is what the total-force concept is all about.

Comments of Vice Admiral Robert F. Dunn, Former Chief of Naval Air Reserve, about the Experience and Capabilities of Reserve P-3 Crews and Naval Air Reservists in General:

"I soon concluded that the only regulars who didn't appreciate the reserves were those who had never operated with Naval Air Reservists. They were extremely good at everything they did, winning competitons and garnering kudos from every quarter.

"One reason they did so well, of course, was their experience. The reserve airmen regularly outperformed their active-duty counterparts, even while flying older aircraft against the brand-new equipment operated by the active forces. An example of this came to light when I flew with VP-62, a Naval Air Reserve patrol squadron at NAS Jacksonville, Florida. VP-62 flew older P-3B Orions at the time, and outperformed the regulars with their P-3C Update series time and time again. No wonder. The skipper had been in the same squadron for fourteen years. The flight engineer had been there for twenty-two years! They easily made up for lack of sophisticated state-of-the-art equipment with motivation, experience, and maturity. But maturity and experience are not unique to VP-62; they are part and parcel of the entire Naval Air Reserve. As soon as I came to this realization, I proceeded to marshall it to the advantage of the whole enterprise."

Transport Squadrons

Although perhaps not as glamorous as the tactical air squadrons, the Naval Air Reserve's transport community has done as much as any reserve component to demonstrate the value of the reserve and the viability of the total-force concept. The program started modestly but has developed to a point where reserve aircraft now provide virtually all the navy's internal airlift capability. Flying modern C-9B aircraft, the VR

The C-118B was arguably the most employed aircraft in the entire Naval Air Reserve from the late '60s through the early '80s. No reservist who served for any length of time escaped riding one of the big, four-engined Douglas transports. Unpressurized, the Skymasters usually flew below 10,000 feet and were subjected to whatever bumps and thermals that existed. But the aircraft was reliable and able to carry whatever could be put into it. This VR-53 Skymaster waits on the NAS Jacksonville ramp in November 1973. (*Courtesy of Nick Williams*)

NAS Atlanta's transport squadrons flew the workhorse Douglas C-54 pictured above before transitioning to C-118s. Following reorganization and the establishment of VR-46, the squadron's 118s operated from NAS Atlanta until the mid-'80s. VR-46 was the last squadron to operate the C-118, retiring the venerable aircraft from navy service in February 1985. (*Courtesy of Nick Williams*)

squadrons transport active-duty and reserve personnel and equipment literally worldwide.

The establishment of a reserve transport capability was part of the original reserve reorganization plan promulgated in 1970. Four squadrons, all flying C-118B aircraft, were organized and based as follows: VR-51, NAS Alameda; VR-52, NAS Willow Grove; VR-53, NAS Memphis; and VR-54, NAS New Orleans. Each squadron also had independent detachments located around the United States to provide more efficient

This VR-51 Skymaster was photographed on final approach to NAS Atsugi, Japan, in the summer of 1975. Flight crews in VR squadrons logged thousands of hours on long flights in the 118s. *(Courtesy of Nick Williams)*

transport services. The detachments, all flying C-118s, were located as follows:

VR-51	NAS Whidbey Island, WA; NAS Glenview, IL
VR-52	NAF Detroit, MI; NAF Washington, DC
VR-53	NAS Dallas, TX
VR-54	NAS Atlanta, GA

The C-118B was a workhorse that more than earned its keep for the navy. It could not compare to jets, however, in terms of payload, range, speed, or passenger comfort. In 1976, the reserve entered a whole new world of service capability with the establishment of C-9 squadrons at NAS Alameda and NAS Norfolk (VR-55 and VR-56). In 1977 two more C-9 squadrons were commissioned, VR-57 and VR-58 at NAS North Island, California, and NAS Jacksonville, Florida, respectively.

Eventually all the C-118s were replaced. The VR-52 detachment at Washington traded its C-118s for turboprop C-131Hs acquired from the District of Columbia National Guard in December 1978. (The detachment was renamed VR-48 in 1980.) In September 1982, VR-53 Det. Dallas, VR-53, Memphis, and VR-51 Det. Whidbey Island were disestablished. In their place, VR-59, VR-60, and VR-61 were established at the same locations, flying C-9s. In June 1982, VR-51 completed its transition to C-9s. The last C-118 in the navy was transferred from VR-46, NAS Atlanta, in 1985.

With the passage from props to jets, the Naval Air Reserve transport squadrons entered a new era of capability. They accomplished their logistics missions so successfully and efficiently that all active-duty C-9s were transferred to reserve force squadrons, and the entire navy internal airlift responsibility was assumed by the Naval Air Reserve. VR reservists have met that responsibility completely and proved their worth time and

NAS Atlanta's VR-46 mechs attend to maintenance on a "118 recip." This photo was taken in late 1984 just before the last C-118s were retired from the Naval Air Reserve at Atlanta. *(Photo by Don Linn)*

Crewmen load a VR-58 C-9 at NAS Cecil Field. The C-9 offers great flexibility in its load-carrying capability and can be quickly configured for either cargo or passenger missions. *(Photo by Peter B. Mersky)*

time again. For example, reservists responded during the hectic times in October 1983 that saw the outbreak of war in Grenada, while on the other side of the Atlantic marines were bombed in their barracks in Beirut, Lebanon. Reserve C-9s from VR-56 and VR-58 carried the Grenada invasion force commander, Rear Admiral Joseph Metcalf, and his staff into the Point Saline Airfield. These were the first fixed-wing aircraft to land at the Cuban-built field during the Grenada operation. VR-58 crews also flew the Cuban prisoners captured during the invasion to Mexico where they were eventually repatriated. Only a few days later VR-56 was called on to transport wounded marines home from the bombing in Lebanon. And all this was in addition to normal transportation services

The VFC squadrons fly the A-4F and the TA-4J such as this one assigned to VFC-13. *(Photo by LCDR Chuck Nangle, VFC-13)*

Like VR, the VC mission proved to be one ideally suited for the Naval Air Reserve. Here two TA-4Js of VC-12 pose over the nation's capital after returning from a support mission for VFP-206. The reserve's ability to fly the VC mission successfully and economically enabled the navy to decommission all active-duty, U.S.-based fleet VC squadrons. The VC squadrons were later redesignated VFC.

VFC-12 A-4Fs operate out of Naval Station Roosevelt Roads, PR. As part of their service mission, the VFC squadrons stage detachments regularly and frequently at sites throughout the United States, Canada, and the Caribbean.

going on back home! The Naval Air Reserve C-9s make hundreds of flights a month, and every flight is a constant reminder and highly visible example of the important role reservists play in today's "One Navy."

Comments of Vice Admiral P. N. Charbonnet, Former Chief of Naval Air Reserve, Concerning the Reserve C-9 Program:

"The first, and one of the most important, crises of my tour as reserve commander happened in the mid-seventies when the secretary of defense directed the navy to divest its organic airlift capability and transfer the mission and assets to the air force. I had served in the Sixth Fleet as commander, Fleet Air Mediterranean during various periods of military confrontation when our naval forces responded to escalating defense conditions. Internal [organic] airlift (C-118s, C-130s, C-9s, C-2s, C-1s) proved absolutely essential and critical to Sixth Fleet capability to perform its mission, and I recall several occasions when reserve C-118s and fleet C-130/C-2s saved us. Naturally, there was a political aspect to this, which involved both the Congress and Department of Defense. We did everything we could to keep our VR squadrons, and ultimately prevailed over the secretary of defense's decision, thanks in major part to House Armed Services Chairman F. Edward Hebert, who was always a strong sponsor for the Naval Air Reserve and a close friend."

Fleet Services

Fleet composite squadrons are another excellent example of reserve utilization. VFC-12 and VFC-13, based at NAS Oceana and NAS Miramar, respectively, provide a wide variety of flight services to the fleet and reserve forces. These services range from towing banners to radar-tracking exercises to air-to-air adversary flights. The ability of VC-12 and -13 to carry out these missions enabled the active-duty navy to eliminate its VC squadrons based in the continental United States in the late seventies. Subsequently, the VC squadrons became so proficient in their adversary role that demand for their services resulted in a higher percentage of their mission being devoted to air-combat maneuvering. The squadron designations were changed from VC to VFC in 1988 to reflect this change in priorities.

HORIZONTAL INTEGRATION: EQUALITY FOR THE RESERVE

As the 1980s began, everything looked positive for the Naval Air Reserve—at least superficially. Never had it been more capable, better funded, or as ready to mobilize. What's more, reserve units were making real contributions to active-duty forces on a daily basis. Yet all was not right. For all the equipment improvements that had been made, there were still major shortcomings that seriously hampered the ability to mobilize, especially the TACAIR squadrons.

The attack squadrons, for instance, had upgraded to A-7Bs, but serious engine problems arose in the early '80s that significantly affected aircraft

The Naval Air Reserve Force's hardware continued to improve as later-model F-4s replaced earlier F-4Bs. Here Phantoms from each of the reserve carrier air wings' fighter squadrons fly formation with a TA-4J from VC-13, the Pacific Fleet reserve adversary squadron, during the annual air-wing deployment to Fallon, Nevada. *(Courtesy of Peter Mersky)*

availability. For example, as of June 1983, only twenty-two of the reserve's seventy-seven Corsairs were flyable because of engine shortages. The fleet was flying A-7Es with Rolls-Royce TF-41 engines, but A-7B Pratt and Whitney TF-30 engines were plagued by shortages due to out-of-production components and engine sales to foreign countries.

The fighter squadrons had moved to later F-4 models such as the F-4N and S, but the Phantoms were 1950s technology and feeling their age. A problem also existed mixing old reserve aircraft with new fleet aircraft in the event of a mobilization. The F-4s required a launch bridle and holdback gear for catapult launches, while newer fleet aircraft used a nose-tow system. It's not hard to visualize the operational and safety problems that could arise if catapult crews, unfamiliar with the bridle-launch equipment, were forced to mix nose-tow and bridle launches during a mobilization. An even greater problem would be supplying the spare parts for the older reserve aircraft and otherwise supporting aircraft that had little in common with the fleet equipment.

The hard truth was that if the nation truly wanted an immediate mobilization capability, the reserve had to have the same aircraft and equipment as the fleet. This concept went against the traditional practice of supplying the reserve with fleet leftovers, a policy that had been in place since the reserve's beginning. Just "because we've always done it that way" wasn't good enough this time for some progressive thinkers who realized the value of the Naval Air Reserve and the need for modern equipment. Old concepts die hard, however, and convincing Congress and the regular navy that reservists should share front-line equipment would not be easy. The reserve needed a champion of their cause in high places, and they found one in Secretary of the Navy John Lehman.

Secretary Lehman, a Naval Air Reservist himself (A-6 bombardier/navigator), realized the importance of a ready reserve, its need for current equipment, and the value of the Naval Air Reserve to the overall defense effort. Mr. Lehman aggressively pursued the concept of

A VA-204 A-7B is pictured aboard the USS *Eisenhower* during carrier quals in September 1985. A serious shortage of TF-30 engines significantly hampered reserve force A-7 squadrons during the early '80s. This was only one example of degraded readiness caused by the basic problem—incompatability with fleet components—that plagued Naval Air Reserve Force squadrons until horizontal integration became a reality.

The ground crew salutes as Commander Dave Strong taxis his RF-8G for the Crusader's final flight on 30 March, 1987. The retirement of this classic aircraft marked the end of an era for many navy fighter pilots and, at the same time, moved the Naval Air Reserve closer to its goal of transition to fleet-compatible carrier air wings. *(Photo by Peter Mersky)*

Two F-4S's from VF-202 refuel from a VAK-208 Skywarrior during a "cruise" at NAS Fallon, Nevada. The F-4S was the latest Phantom model, but it was not an optimum aircraft for mobilization because of the difficulty that aircraft carriers would have supporting an aircraft no longer in the active air-wing inventory. *(VFP-206 photo)*

The Douglas A-3 Skywarrior, originally designed in 1949 for the carrier heavy-attack mission and nuclear weapons delivery, is one of the venerable naval aircraft of all time. "Whales" were modified to perform a variety of missions and were configured for the (VAQ) electronic-warfare role in the 1970s. The KA-3B served as the navy's only in-flight refueling and long-range over-water "pathfinder" throughout the '80s. These "tankers" from VAK-208 were photographed over San Francisco Bay shortly before the squadron was disestablished on 30 September 1989. *(Photo by CDR D. Kisela)*

"horizontal integration": giving reservists aircraft and training identical to their fleet counterparts, enabling the reserve to mesh interchangeably with the fleet. Horizontal integration was an absolute necessity if the concept of the total-force navy was ever to come to fruition.

Comments of Rear Admiral Frederick Palmer, CNAVRES 1978–1982, on Secretary of the Navy John Lehman and Horizontal Integration:

"Horizontal integration was a major change for which I got most of the credit but which was generated largely by the young secretary of the navy, John Lehman, himself a drilling reservist. I recall our first meeting at a banquet. He mentioned that he was a lieutenant commander in the Naval Reserve. I said I was the Chief *of the Naval Reserve, and he jumped up and saluted me. That didn't happen again.*

"Secretary Lehman saw the necessity of getting out of the give-the-old-airplanes-to-the-reserves syndrome, and getting reservists into the identical cockpits they would have if they were mobilized. If you want to have an effective Naval Air Reserve, you have to have identical, fleet-comparable equipment. It's as simple as that. I think that many fleet aviators did not truly understand that, particularly when they saw the reserves getting new F/A-18s.

I think Secretary Lehman basically understood what was needed, and I felt the same. It was easy for me to work with his program. His suggestions were not always popular with the regulars, but in the larger view, toward sustained operations in a protracted situation, you need a ready reserve. I speak from experience, having been recalled to active duty in

Horizontal integration became a reality when VF-301 transitioned to F-14s in 1984. Here a Tomcat from VF-301 maneuvers near NAS El Centro, California. *(Photo by George Hall)*

Both reserve VAW squadrons, VAW-78 and VAW-88, now operate the advanced E-2C, the navy's newest and most capable airborne early-warning aircraft. This "Hummer" from CVWR-30's VAW-88 at NAS Miramar is over the southern Andes Mountains en route to Bahia Blanca, Argentina, for exercise "UNITAS" in September 1989. *(Photo by LCDR Nordmeyer)*

Korea in 1950. You can see very well the importance of having a ready reserve capable of manning ships and squadrons in the fleet during a crisis."

Secretary Lehman's dynamic leadership and a generally more favorable attitude in the U.S. towards defense spending enabled horizontal integration to begin in the early '80s. In June 1983, VAW-78 accepted its first E-2C, the navy's most advanced airborne early-warning aircraft. It didn't take long for the new concept of horizontal integration to pay dividends. In March 1984, VAW-126, a fleet E-2 squadron deployed off Beirut aboard the USS *John F. Kennedy* (CV 67), needed aircrew assistance. Their aircrews had been flying around-the-clock missions off the coast of Lebanon for months and fatigue was setting in. VAW-78 received the call on a Friday afternoon in Norfolk, Virginia, with a request for flight-crew support. Three days later, two reserve pilots and two NFOs were flying missions for VAW-126 off Lebanon. This was what horizontal integration was all about.

In October 1984, VF-301 at NAS Miramar accepted its first F-14, and VA-205 transitioned into the A-7E. The next year, 1985, was an even more significant year as VA-303 was redesignated VFA-303 and accepted the first eight F/A-18 Hornets for the Naval Air Reserve. The delivery of F/A-18s to the reserve was a milestone from several standpoints. It was the first time a reserve squadron had ever received a new aircraft before all active-duty squadrons had transitioned to it. More importantly, it also represented the navy's firm commitment to horizontal integration and the "One-Navy" concept.

Comments of Rear Admiral Rinard about the Reserve Force's Acquisition of F/A-18s:

"One of the continuing questions I was asked at the Tailhook Symposiums was why the Naval Air Reserve should transition into the latest fleet aircraft, the F/A-18, prior to all the active forces getting them. The argument was that if you're going into combat, you'll take your active forces first, and they should have the very latest equipment.

"I think the F/A-18 is a good example of horizontal integration. A lot of the people who have contrary opinions forget that this was well thought out prior to making that decision.

"If you go back and look at it, we didn't preclude any active squadron from making their transition within their scheduled time frame. What we did was to sandwich in one reserve squadron at NAS Lemoore, with no additional support equipment required, such as AIMD [aircraft intermediate maintenance department], which is the major portion of the support organization. Had we transitioned another fleet squadron, there wasn't a carrier capable of deploying it.

"We did not do a full-blown transition to the F/A-18 by the Naval Air Reserve, and we did not impact the Fleet Replacement Squadron with having to take a full squadron of people. We only shuffled a few people in and then we pulled back and did our own training.

"To my knowledge, not one active-duty aviator was denied transition to F/A-18s because the Naval Air Reserve got a squadron. Until support equipment arrives and the aircraft carrier is outfitted, the fleet can't afford to have the aircraft. As it turns out, reserve squadrons will be the last to completely phase out the A-7s, when the carriers are no longer capable of supporting them."

Comments of John Lehman, Former Secretary of the Navy, about the Role of Reservists:

"There has not been a major postwar crisis where Naval Air Reservists have not voluntarily augmented the forward deployed navy: In the Persian Gulf, in the carriers off Beirut, and in the Gulf of Sidra. The Naval Air Reserve is filled with people whose greatest wish and excitement comes from supporting the active navy and easing their burdens. The last thing a Naval Air Reservist would want to do is to increase the burdens or

VFA-303 accepted its first F/A-18 on 19 October 1984. Secretary of the Navy the Honorable John Lehman, a "selected reservist" as well, is greeted by Commander Naval Air Reserve Force, Rear Admiral Tommy F. Rinard (back to camera), upon arrival for the official ceremony at NAS Lemoore, CA. At left is the squadron's commanding officer, Commander Bob Greathouse.

compete for the resources of the men and women deployed with the fleet."

The tactical reserve air wings received a big boost in capability with the transition of VA-304 to A-6E and KA-6D (aerial refueling version) aircraft in 1989. VA-205, NAS Atlanta, followed suit the following year. This transition gave the reserve air wings a medium attack capability for the first time in their history.

Just as important to the Naval Air Reserve was the introduction of another type of Intruder in 1989. VAQ-309 traded in its obsolete EA-6As for state-of-the-art EA-6Bs. Shortly thereafter, VAQ-209 from CVWR-20 began its transition to Prowlers, and also moved its home base from NAS Norfolk to NAF Washington, D.C. Navy experience in Vietnam and Libya vividly demonstrated the importance of effective electronic countermeasures. Sophisticated radar defense systems demand equally advanced ECM capabilities, and in the EA-6B, the Naval Air Reserve has the newest and the best.

By the beginning of 1991 the reserve carrier air wings had finally attained a composition that truly mirrored their active-duty counterparts.

A VF-302 Tomcat "gets a drink" from a tanker. VF-302 and its sister squadron, VF-301, attached to CVWR-30, are based at NAS Miramar with "CAG-30." *(Photo by George Hall)*

VFA-303 was the first Naval Air Reserve squadron to transition to the F/A-18. Commissioned in July 1970, the squadron traces its roots back to the last days of WW II. In 1948 the then VF-876 flew the famous Grumman F6F Hellcat before it transitioned to the attack mission and the A-4 Skyhawk in the late '60s. They were also the first Naval Air Reserve squadron to transition to the A-7A Corsair II.

An EA-6A of VAQ-209 fires a HARM anti-radiation missile during a training exercise. Both reserve VAQ squadrons transitioned to the four-place EA-6B Prowler in 1989 and 1990.

VAQ-209 transitioned from the EA-6A to the EA-6B in mid-1990 and, at the same time, moved from NAS Norfolk to NAF Washington, D.C., at Andrews Air Force Base. In this photo the squadron's TAR officer-in-charge, Commander Steve Christopher, gets the "keys" from Captain James Aldrich of the Defense Plant Representative's Office at Grumman Corporation.

Another distinction for the Naval Air Reserve occurred when the last production Orion was delivered to a reserve force squadron. Rear Admiral Richard K. Chambers, Commander Naval Air Reserve Force, accepted the aircarft in ceremonies at Lockheed's Palmdale, California, Plant Ten on 17 April 1990. The aircraft, an Update III, was assigned to VP-91.

The EA-6B offered a considerable upgrade of ECM capabilities for the Naval Air Reserve's two VAQ squadrons. The Prowler's air frame is similar to that of the A-6 Intruder but has been lengthened 40-inches to accommodate the two additional flight crew members and the advanced electronic warfare package. *(Photo by George Hall)*

On the 75th anniversary of the Naval Air Reserve, the composition of CVWR-20 and -30 was as shown in table 3.

Table 3. Composition of CVWR-30/-20 in 1991

Squadron	Home Station	Type Aircraft
VF-301/201	NAS Miramar / NAS Dallas	F-14A
VF-302/202	NAS Miramar / NAS Dallas	F-14A
VFA-303/VFA-203	NAS Lemoore / NAS Cecil	F/A-18A
VA-304/VA-205	NAS Alameda / NAS Atlanta	A-6E & KA-6D
VFA-305/VFA-204	NAS Pt. Mugu / NAS New Orleans	F/A-18A
VAW-88/78	NAS Miramar / NAS Norfolk	E-2C
VAQ-309/209	NAS Whidbey / NAF Washington	EA-6B

Maritime Patrol

Aircraft modernization in the '80s was not limited to tactical aircraft. The navy's state-of-the-art antisubmarine aircraft, the P-3C Update III model, was delivered to Reserve Patrol Squadron (VP) 62 at NAS Jacksonville, Florida. Additionally, all the other reserve P-3 squadron aircraft had the TAC/NAV modification incorporated, which greatly enhanced their mission capability.

Rotary Wing

The rotary wing community also saw many exciting additions to their inventory. In keeping with the goal of horizontal integration, HS-84 transitioned from SH-3D to SH-2F aircraft and formed the reserve's first LAMPS (Light Airborne Multi-Purpose System) at NAS North Island in

90

A VP-64 P-3A, TACNAV MOD Orion like this one flew the navy's last East Coast operational "Alpha" flight in March 1990. The squadron transitioned to the "Bravo" soon after. The Naval Air Reserve has operated a variety of Lockheed patrol aircraft, beginning with the famous Hudsons and followed by the Ventura, Harpoon, and Neptune.

A ground crewman directs a reserve P-3 at NAS Bermuda. Many reserve Orion squadrons go to Bermuda for training cruises to augment the fleet ASW unit, and to take advantage of the excellent flying weather. Reserve VP squadrons routinely assume active-duty patrol commitments and are tasked for operational missions on a regular basis. *(Photo by JOC Russ Egnor)*

Horizontal integration brought many advances to the Naval Air Reserve as its missions were redefined and expanded. A milestone for the patrol community was achieved in late 1987 when VP-62 accepted a brand new Update III Orion. This was the first time in the history of the Naval Air Reserve that "right-off-the-line" equipment was delivered to a reserve squadron.

The establishment of HM-18 in 1986 gave the Naval Air Reserve its first capability in the aerial minesweeping mission. HM-18 at NAS Norfolk and HM-19 at NAS Alameda operate the RH-53D.

Three HSL helicopter squadrons were formed over several years in the late '70s and early '80s to give the Naval Air Reserve a capability in the important LAMPS mission. Here an SH-2F from HSL-74 prepares to launch from the flight deck of her frigate. The squadrons began transition to the SH-2G in 1991.

The versatility of the HH-60H enabled the Naval Air Reserve to combine the HC and the HAL missions. Here an HH-60H from HCS-4 at NAS Norfolk lowers a man to a utility landing craft.

1984. The LAMPS helicopters fly off frigate-type ships engaging in anti-submarine warfare and antiship surveillance and targeting. In subsequent years, HS-74 gave up its SH-3Ds to accept SH-2Fs and become HSL-74, at South Weymouth, Massachusetts, and HSL-94 was established at NAS Willow Grove, Pennsylvania, giving the reserve a major capability in the LAMPS mission.

Another important step in the horizontal integration program was the establishment of HM-18 at NAS Norfolk in October 1986. HM-18, flying the RH-53D, became the reserve's first airborne minesweeping (officially airborne mine countermeasures) squadron. Mining of the Persian Gulf in 1987/88 demonstrated the urgent need for a quick-reaction airborne minesweeping capability. And under the total-force concept, where there's a mission, there should be a reserve component to support it. A second AMCM squadron designated HM-19 was established in January 1989 at NAS Alameda, giving the reserve a total of ten AMCM helicopters.

Another exciting development in the helicopter community was the November 1988 transition of HAL-5 to a new mission and a new aircraft. HAL-5 became Helicopter Combat Support Squadron Special (HCS) 5, and was assigned a new aircraft, the HH-60H. The squadron was created to combine the missions of HC and HAL squadrons. With the increased capability of the HH-60H helicopter, the new HCS squadron could provide for the strike rescue mission as well as support navy SEAL and Special Forces teams. The commissioning of HCS-5 and its sister squad-

An SH-3G from HS-75 approaches the carrier *Eisenhower* during a CVWR-20 training cruise in July 1989. HS-75 and HS-85 transitioned to this aircraft from the SH-3D in 1989 and 1990, making the squadrons compatible with fleet HS units. *(Courtesy Peter B. Mersky)*

The Naval Air Reserve significantly increased its cargo transport capability with the acceptance of the C-130T in June 1991. The aircraft are assigned to VR-54, a new squadron based at NAS New Orleans.

This C-20 is assigned to VR-48 at NAF Washington, D.C. The C-20 replaced the C-131H in 1990, and is an efficient, comfortable aircraft for missions that don't require a large plane.

ron HCS-4 in 1989 also represented a milestone in that it was the first time an aircraft had been designed and procured specifically for the reserves. Delivery of the first HH-60H began in 1989 with a total of eighteen scheduled for delivery to two naval reserve HCS squadrons. The HCS program is another excellent example of the total-force concept.

Transport

Two new aircraft entered reserve service in the VR community as the 1990s began. VR-48, based at NAF Washington, D.C., retired its C-131H aircraft and acquired the C-20 for its personnel transport mission. The C-20 is the military version of the Gulfstream-American G-4 corporate jet. This jet gives the reserve force the flexibility to provide efficient transport service for the many VR missions that don't require a large aircraft.

Another new aircraft for the reserve force was introduced in June 1991. VR-54 was established at NAS New Orleans, flying the Lockheed C-130T. The *Hercules* has been a proven workhorse for years with other military branches, and its addition to the Naval Air Reserve greatly increases the force's cargo-carrying capability.

Efficient and timely logistic support is critical to any mobilization. Horizontal integration would not be complete without similar aircraft modernization in the transport community. With the C-9, C-20, and C-130, the reserve force has the modern tools necessary to provide logistic support during routine operations and during mobilizations.

Profile of Former Secretary of the Navy John Lehman

Secretary of the Navy John H. Lehman, SECNAV between 1981 and 1988, has to be given much of the credit for the modernization of the Naval Air Reserve and the expansion of its role. Secretary Lehman strongly believed in the reservists' capability and felt their role should be increased in the total-force concept for our nation's defense. During his tenure as SECNAV, reserve squadrons started flying F/A-18s, P-3Cs, F-14As, E-2Cs, and other late-model aircraft. His dynamic leadership and ability to convince Congress and the navy about the value of a capable air reserve set the stage for the ongoing modernization of the reserve force.

Mr. Lehman was appointed secretary of the navy by President Ronald Reagan on 23 January 1981. He was confirmed by the Senate less than a week later and took the oath of office on 5 February. He was one of the youngest men ever to be appointed to that position.

Mr. Lehman earned a B.S. in international relations in 1964 at St. Joseph's College. He continued his education at Cambridge University in England as an Earhart Fellow. He graduated in 1967, receiving a B.A. with Honours, Law and an M.A. in Internal Law and Diplomacy. In 1974, Mr. Lehman earned a Ph.D in International Relations from the University of Pennsylvania.

Mr. Lehman accepted a direct commission as an ensign in the Naval Reserve in January 1968. He subsequently was designated a naval flight officer (bombardier-navigator) and regularly performed active-duty training with VA-42, the A-6 fleet replacement squadron. He now holds the rank of captain, USNR.

Prior to his appointment as secretary of the navy, Mr. Lehman was a staff member of the Foreign Policy Institute at the University of Pennsylvania, a special counsel and senior staff member to Dr. Henry Kissinger on the National Security Council, a delegate to the Mutual Balanced Force Reductions in Vienna, and Deputy Director of the U.S. Arms Control and Disarmament Agency. Immediately prior to his government service, he was president of Abington, Corp., a management firm that specializes in defense matters. Following his tour as SECNAV, Mr. Lehman took a position as a managing director of Paine Webber Corporation in New York.

Mr. Lehman continues to participate in the Naval Air Reserve, where his service both to the navy and the reserve program is highly valued.

REINFORCING AND SUSTAINING UNITS

To most observers, squadrons and aircraft represent the sum total of the Naval Air Reserve force. Unquestionably they are the most conspicuous part of the Naval Air Reserve, but just as important to the navy's total-force mission are the thousands of men and women serving "just off the flight line" in reserve components known as reinforcing and sustaining units. These units perform a variety of functions, but most have one characteristic in common: they do not "own" aircraft. Reservists in most of the reinforcing units operate aircraft assigned to fleet or reserve force squadrons, while those assigned to the sustaining units support flight operations in non-flying billets.

Sustaining units in particular are tasked with training individuals for a variety of aviation support roles. In almost all instances, individuals

Members of Reserve Unit CV-62, USS *Independence* 0389, posed for a group photo on the flight deck forward of the island while the ship was in port at NAS North Island during annual training. "Indy" is augmented by three units that drill at NAVAIRES Whidbey Island, NAF Washington, D.C., and NAVAIRES Pt. Mugu, California. More than three hundred officers and enlisted billets are combined in the three units.

assigned to these components possess special skills, proficiencies, and "designations" gained through prior active service. They provide everyday support for their gaining command (where they would report in event of mobilization) while maintaining a vital pool of back-up manpower that can be called upon in event of national emergency. Sustaining units exist for a variety of active-duty commands, including the naval intelligence program, navy medicine, aerology, aviation maintenance, aeronautical engineering, aircraft carriers, air stations, and aviation staff support, to mention a few. The contribution of these units to the navy's total mission is significant. Without the programmed participation of individual reservists assigned to these units, numerous operational commitments would not be met and major exercises could not take place.

The following examples of reinforcing and sustaining units are not all-inclusive, but they do give an indication of the variety and importance of the missions performed by these units.

SQUADRON AUGMENT UNITS

The role of squadron augment units (SAUs) is just what the name implies: to augment active-duty squadrons in time of need with trained and qualified—in aircraft type—reserve flight crews and maintenance personnel who would be immediately available to bring the manning levels of active-force squadrons to wartime complements.

The SAU program, conceived in the late '70s and inaugurated in the early '80s, has several variations. Some SAUs are assigned to reserve-force squadrons and fly their aircraft. Other SAUs are affiliated with active-duty fleet replacement squadrons (FRS)—the squadrons that train active-duty aviators to fly fleet aircraft. Reserve aviators assigned to these

While the Naval Air Reserve has no S-3s in its current inventory, these reservists from Squadron Augment Unit VS-0294, the "Moonlighters," operate fleet aircraft assigned to the West Coast S-3 Fleet Replacement Squadron, VS-41. The close working relationship between VS-41 and its reserve augment unit has provided benefits for both the reserve and active-duty units. This group shot shows the first reserve crews to carrier qualify in the S-3.

Caught at the exact moment of engagement, a VS-27 S-3A flown by a reserve crew traps during a CQ period off the East Coast. As the fleet replacement training squadron for the "Vikings" on the East Coast, VS-27 "loans" its aircraft to VS-0174, its reserve augment unit, drilling aboard NAS Cecil Field, FL. *(Photo by Peter B. Mersky)*

SAUs fly FRS aircraft and the aircraft of the active-duty squadron that they would be mobilized to when activated.

The SAU program proved to be beneficial for both reserve and active-duty commands. Flying active-duty aircraft opened up new training opportunities for reserve flight crews, while the active-duty squadrons took advantage of the experience and proficiency of the reservists. Most, if not all, of the pilots and NFOs assigned to the fleet replacement squadron SAUs are highly experienced in that type of equipment. Many were FRS instructors prior to leaving active duty. These highly experienced crews could therefore step right in and help by providing qualified instructors to the FRS. At one time in the mid-eighties, active-duty staffing was so low in VA-128, the A-6E FRS, that the squadron's training effort would have been severely degraded had it not been for the support of VA-0689, the West Coast A-6 squadron augment unit.

Fleet squadrons have also benefited from the SAU program. Since reservists in the SAU also fly fleet aircraft from the squadrons that hold their mobilization billet, they offer the fleet an immediate source of additional manpower. On more than one occasion, reserve crews from the SAU have gone on special active duty with their assigned squadron to assist in meeting operational and training commitments. The SAU program is a good example of a new approach to cooperative training that benefits reserve and active-duty forces alike.

A variation of the squadron augment unit is the master augment unit (MAU). The P-3 community has established MAUs at NAS Brunswick,

Reserve flight crews began flying the A-6E with VA-128, the West Coast fleet replacement squadron for the Intruder, at NAS Whidbey Island, WA. The Squadron Augment Unit, VA-0689, has logged hundreds of flights that support both the reserve and fleet training syllabus.

Maine, and NAS Moffett Field, California. The MAU is a cross between a reserve-force squadron and a squadron augment unit. MAU aircraft are assigned to the squadron (on a sub-custody basis from the fleet), but the squadron would not mobilize as an integral unit. Its members train as a squadron in fleet equipment (P-3Cs), but mobilize individually to fleet squadrons to augment those units in a time of need.

The SAU/MAU program has been characterized by the present Naval Air Reserve leadership as one that "recovers the investment" of time, training, and money made by the navy. The 600 pilots and NFOs and the 1,200 enlisted personnel assigned to these units were trained at considerable expense. Keeping these airmen trained, current, and available means that this expensive investment is still paying dividends. The SAUs and MAUs are meeting the needs and expectations for real time, cost-effective training for both the Naval Air Reserve and the active navy.

AVIATION SUPPORT PROGRAMS

Many Naval Air Reservists are members of units that, while not directly involved in flying, provide support for reserve and active-duty flight programs. These, like all Naval Air Reserve units, are designed to meet wartime mobilization needs. Units in the flight support program include flight medical, mobile maintenance, antisubmarine operations centers, tactical air control, and naval oceanography.

Flight Medical

The Flight Medical Program has more than a thousand doctors, dentists, flight surgeons, aerospace medical personnel, medical corpsmen, and nurses trained and ready for mobilization. Their purpose is to provide qualified support to naval air stations, Navy Medical Command hospitals and clinics, and to the Fourth Marine Air Wing (Marine Reserve Air Wing). In addition to their fleet mobilization requirements, reservists in the medical units provide services to drilling Naval Air Reservists such as flight physicals, annual physical examinations, and emergency medical care.

The importance of the medical units was graphically underscored during Operation Desert Shield/Storm. Doctors, nurses, corpsmen, and other medical specialists were among the first to be mobilized to meet the needs of the nation following the invasion of Kuwait. Their ability to fill gaps left by active-duty medical personnel deployed overseas was a critical factor in the nation's ability to react to a foreign threat.

Mobile Maintenance Facilities

The advanced-base functional component (ABFC)/P-3 Mobile Maintenance Facility (MMF) is the navy's premier program of its kind. Designed to mobilize within forty-eight hours, these units provide autonomous, remote maintenance support for P-3 aircraft. The MMFs and ABFCs are commissioned units that travel in mobile van units, transportable by aircraft such as the C-141, to support maintenance at remote sites. The vans contain high-value P-3 bench-support, test equipment, and supplies that enable maritime patrol aircraft to operate from remote sites for sustained periods.

The mobile vans of Advance Base Functional Component Mobile Maintenance Facility "Hotel", NAF Washington, D.C., provide critical maintenance capability in support of maritime patrol remote site operations. This 1990 photograph shows the unit's vans being moved for loading aboard an air force C-141.

This Moffett-based P-3C is operated by the NAS Moffett VP Master Augment Unit, one of the two VP "MAUs." The MAUs have aircraft assigned to them, but the flight crews they train mobilize to various fleet squadrons on an individual basis.

Antisubmarine Warfare Operations Centers

No less traveled are the thirteen Antisubmarine Warfare Operations Center (ASWOC) units that provide trained command, communication, and control personnel to fleet and patrol wing ASWOCs. Like other Naval Air Reserve programs, these are special units manned by personnel with an extensive background in all phases of antisubmarine warfare (ASW) operations. Members assigned to these units participate with their gaining commands on a regular basis at sites around the world providing critical support in the ASW arena.

Tactical Air Control

Tactical air control units include four TACRON (tactical air control squadrons) and two TACGRUs (tactical air control groups). These units are composed of people trained to coordinate aircraft operations in support of amphibious operations. In addition they provide training for the close air support mission of both navy and Marine Corps active forces.

Naval Oceanography

Additional direct aviation support comes from the Naval Oceanography Reserve Program (NORP) units. From this program we get the weather specialists—the meteorologists—without whom flight operations are seriously jeopardized. There are eighteen "weather" units managed by the Naval Air Reserve.

OTA1 Mary Rodney (left) and OTA1 Dianne Larsen-Wolfe of Anti-Submarine Warfare Operational Control unit 0389 at NAVAIRES Whidbey Island are typical of many Naval Air Reservists assigned to one of more than 440 reinforcing and sustaining units. Trained and experienced, they allow the navy to augment the active force with a cadre of specialists who have skills and proficiencies to perform a wide range of complex tasks.

ASHORE AND AFLOAT SUPPORT PROGRAMS

Equally important to the Naval Air Reserve and the active navy are the programs that provide highly trained, qualified officer and enlisted personnel to the navy's shore-based facilities and aircraft carriers. More than forty-five base and station (NAS, NAF, NAVSTA) units provide a cadre of trained, mobilization-ready personnel to augment naval air stations, naval air facilities, and naval stations. Members of these components are trained to augment fleet activities upon mobilization. In many cases the units are co-located with their gaining commands, so that selected reservists can drill at their mobilization sites with reciprocal benefits to both fleet and reserve commands. The mutual support that derives from this arrangement is a fundamental cornerstone of these types of programs. Reservists integrate directly into every aspect of their command's mission, and, in many instances, become the infusion of manpower and experience required to complete tasks that otherwise might go unfinished. From mess specialists to mechanics, these reservists train with their gaining commands ashore and at sea to hone their skills should their expertise be required to sustain operations around the world.

A similar relationship exists with the thirty-three aviation staff units that augment major aviation staff commands. Like the base and station units, aviation staff units train to provide qualified individuals to fill key staff jobs upon mobilization or recall. Many senior officers with years of experience in naval aviation are assigned to these units.

Under the heading "afloat augmentation" come the aircraft carrier units: CVs, CVNs, and AVT (USS *Lexington*, AVT 16, is the only aircraft carrier assigned a training role). These units train personnel to augment the navy's aircraft carrier crews, giving these ships the extra manpower required to sustain wartime operations. Many of the forty-plus reserve CV units are located along the coasts of the United States and, whenever possible, are situated near their gaining commands. These units typically conduct annual training aboard their assigned ships and frequently perform weekend drills aboard ship, thus maintaining a close relationship with their active-duty counterparts. These units are composed of a relatively small number of officers and senior enlisted and approximately one hundred junior petty officers and airmen.

Naval Air Reserve aerologists perform weekend drills with Naval Oceanographic Reserve Program units at nearly every naval air station across the United States. In this photo Lieutenant Commander Kathryn Sullivan, attached to Naval Oceanographic Reserve Activity 1570, NAS Dallas, checks data on the weather map. In her civilian career Lieutenant Commander Sullivan is an astronaut with the National Aeronautics and Space Administration.

Aviation Intermediate Maintenance Departments reap the benefits of work performed by reservists assigned to NAS, NAF, and NavBase units. Many of them enter the reserve program after one or two fleet enlistments and retain special skills and proficiencies as well as critical designations (NECs). Here AT3 Jerome Wilkerson runs tests on an air navigation "black box" at NAS Willow Grove's AIMD.

ABE3 Chris Johnson, attached to NR CV-62, USS *Independence* 0389, inspects an F/A-18 prior to launch during the unit's first ACDUTRA aboard the carrier in early 1990.

Afloat augment Units, such as the carrier group components, support eight fleet carrier groups—four Atlantic and four Pacific. Here the commanding officer of CARGRU 0466, NAF Washington, D.C., discusses plans for annual training with the XO, training officer, and their program manager.

Flight-deck crews perform what has best been described as a "ballet" as they launch and recover aircraft in the navy's most demanding environment. In this photo a selected reservist attached to CV-41 0176 at NAVAIRES Pt. Mugu works the flight deck during annual training on board ship. *(Photo by Daniel Bayer)*

NAVAL AIR SYSTEMS COMMAND

Some forty Naval Air Systems Command program units are located at eighteen training sites across the United States. Called NAVAIR, these units support the navy's Naval Air Systems Command in the development, testing, procurement, and support of air weapons systems. The nearly 800 officers and enlisted personnel of the Air Systems program train for mobilization at the program headquarters in Washington, D.C., as well as the eighteen NAVAIR field activities.

INTELLIGENCE UNITS

In 1974, the air intelligence and surface intelligence programs were combined to form the Naval Reserve Intelligence Program (NRIP), the largest community of reinforcing and sustaining units in the Naval Reserve. More than 5,000 naval reservists drill in 160 units located at 103 different drill sites, in 19 Reserve Intelligence Areas (RIAs). NRIP members provide support to fifty-five navy and joint commands during drill weekends, active-duty training, and fleet exercises. This support includes replacing active-duty watchstanders, analysis of multi-source intelligence data, and preparation of intelligence studies. NRIP members also assist criminal and fraud investigations and are involved in counterintelligence, counterterrorism, and hostage crisis exercises. The NRIP conducts the Reserve Intelligence Specialist (IS) "A" school, the only "A" school in the Naval Reserve. The school, in conjunction with additional training at fleet intelligence schools, is equivalent to the "A" School training received by active-duty IS's. Over 1,000 reserve IS's have graduated since 1979.

IS2 James Rider (left) and TM2 (SS) Phil Fosterman conduct training at the Naval Reserve IS "A" school at NAF Washington, D.C. Intelligence specialists provide essential, time-critical data analysis to the navy. *(Photo by Peter B. Mersky)*

During joint exercises naval reserve intelligence specialists work hand in hand with members of other services. Here an air force specialist assists a Naval Air Reserve IS as she grades mission film. *(Photo by Peter B. Mersky)*

Former Chief of Naval Reserve Vice Admiral Robert Dunn made the following statement in reference to the Naval Reserve Intelligence Program: "... through my time as Chief of Naval Reserve ... the Reserve Intelligence Command, a Reserve aviation program, soared to new heights of excellence and reputation with the fleet and with the Director of Naval Intelligence."

SPECIAL-PURPOSE SUPPORT

Special-purpose support can best be characterized by the service it provides to the Naval Air Reserve. In most cases the support comes not from units, but from individuals. These reservists are already trained and bring to the Naval Air Reserve and to the active navy a broad range of professional expertise not otherwise available.

Judge advocate general (legal) officers, public-affairs officers, journalists, and chaplains are assigned to various Naval Air Reserve units for administrative purposes but provide services to both the fleet and the Naval Air Reserve. They perform annual training at mobilization sites as well as with specific units when tasked.

Unique to the area of special-purpose support are the units of the Fleet Imaging Command. The personnel that "man-up" these units are the photographers, photojournalists, and audiovisual specialists that keep the image of the Naval Air Reserve before the navy and the world. Two reserve Combat Camera Group units, a PsyOp (psychological operations) group, and two imaging units comprise the Reserve Fleet Imaging Program.

VOLUNTEER TRAINING UNITS (VTU)

The volunteer training units are composed of individual officers and enlisted members who for various reasons are not assigned to squadrons or reinforcing and sustaining units in a pay status. Many veteran reservists join a VTU because they want to remain affiliated with the Naval Air Reserve even though their seniority precludes them from holding a pay billet. Others join the VTU to begin their reserve affiliation while waiting for an opening to occur in a RESFORON or augment unit. VTU members constitute a pool of leadership, experience, and professionalism that remains available to the Naval Air Reserve and the active navy. The thirty-three VTUs in the Naval Air Reserve allow the navy to meet mobilization needs in excess of Selected Air Reserve manning.

The number of reinforcing and sustaining units has remained fairly constant over the years—about 440. But change is inevitable, and as the mission and manpower requirements of the active navy change so will the configuration of the components of the Naval Air Reserve. The only thing that will not change is the important role these unsung heroes play in the mission of the Naval Air Reserve.

Reservists attached to Atlantic Fleet Imaging Units are specialists who provide a wide variety of public affairs and media services to the navy. Unit members often accompany both reserve and fleet components to record activity. Here a motion picture photographer attached to Naval Reserve Atlantic Fleet Audiovisual Unit 193, NAS Willow Grove, films operations at the navy's base in Rota, Spain. *(Photo by WO1 Ed Bailey)*

NAVAL RESERVE AIR BASES AND STATIONS

The reorganization of the Naval Air Reserve in the 1970s resulted in many reserve squadrons relocating to active-duty bases. These moves were in keeping with the new philosophy of the reserve mirroring their fleet counterparts. By moving to active-duty bases, squadrons were located at their mobilization sites and benefited from the supply and intermediate-level maintenance support afforded by an active-duty base. Although Naval Air Reserve bases such as Willow Grove, Pennsylvania, Dallas, Texas, South Weymouth, Massachusetts, Atlanta, Georgia, Glenview, Illinois, and New Orleans, Louisiana, are still active and maintain reserve squadrons, much of Naval Air Reserve history is now being written at active-duty naval air stations such as Miramar, Whidbey Island, Oceana, Moffett, Jacksonville, and Cecil Field. No history of the Naval Air Reserve would be complete, however, without looking at the important role Naval Air Reserve bases and stations have played in the development of reserve aviation.

SQUANTUM, MASSACHUSETTS

If any one air base had to be identified as the birthplace of reserve aviation it would be Squantum, Massachusetts. Located about ten miles south of Boston at the junction of the Neponset River and Dorchester Bay, Squantum was named by Captain Miles Standish after his Indian guide, Squanto. The area he named turned out to be an ideal site for the competitive flying meet the Harvard Aeronautical Association initiated in 1910. The association leased the land for five years and held the first organized competitive scientific and flying tournament in the United States on 10 September 1910.

Early in 1917 the Navy Department recognized the value of the rolling marshland called Squantum and took over 630 acres for defense purposes. The Commonwealth of Massachusetts built a wooden hangar at the site of the Harvard air meets, and the navy established a seaplane base using the new hangar facilities.

In 1923 Congress passed the Naval Reserve Act, which authorized the formation of a few Naval Air Reserve units at those locations where there was sufficient public interest. There was no shortage of interest and enthusiasm among the WW I naval aviators who had returned to the Boston area determined to use the skills they had learned in the war. Accordingly, a "two-unit" base was authorized for the Boston area, and

The Naval Air Reserve's first aviation base, NRAB Squantum, was established near Boston in 1923. The battle in the skies over France during World War I had established the future of the airplane in military operations, and plans to expand air capability included the Naval Air Reserve.

Naval Reserve Air Base (NRAB) Squantum was commissioned. Two seaplane squadrons, VS-4 commanded by Lieutenant Julian D. Ivey, A-F, USNR, and VF-11, led by Lieutenant Paul Ives, A-F, USNR, were organized as a result of the Reserve Act and moved shortly thereafter to NRAB Squantum. The first Naval Air Reserve squadrons were officially in place.

In 1928 the status of reserve aviation was upgraded. An active-duty officer was put in charge of the NRABs, and a new training program was designed to put reserve aviation on equal footing with the regular navy. The facilities at Squantum were improved, the runway lengthened, and a new hangar built to shelter seaplanes previously exposed to the Boston nor'easters. Concurrently, new aircraft—NY-2s, NC-2s, F8Cs, and one OL-9—arrived, making the reserve airplanes comparable to their active-duty counterparts. With the upgraded facilities and aircraft, Squantum became a major training base for the Naval Air Reserve.

When World War II broke out, Squantum was ready to take up the challenge of training the desperately needed naval aviators. By 1943, over 2,300 airmen had completed their primary training at Squantum, filling the skies over New England with their N3N "Yellow Perils."

At the conclusion of WW II, the navy organized the Naval Air Reserve Training Command in an attempt to retain the experience and expertise of the many aviators trained during the war. Squantum NRAB went under the control of the new command, as did twenty other naval reserve air bases. Before long Squantum was actively involved in maintaining the proficiency of its squadrons of reserve aviators. As might be expected, squadrons and personnel from Squantum were among the first called up to meet the Korean crisis.

A lack of space to expand and conflicts with civilian air traffic out of Boston's Logan Airport eventually necessitated a move for naval air reservists. In 1953, the U.S. Naval Air Station at South Weymouth, Massachusetts, was officially recommissioned, and all reserve training at Squantum was transferred to the new facility. Squantum was closed, but its role in the development of the Naval Air Reserve and its position as the "first" Naval Air Reserve base have earned Squantum a special distinction in the history of the Naval Air Reserve.

NRAB Squantum saw a wide variety of aircraft that operated from its runways and seadrome. Pictured here are a DeHavilland floatplane from a Canadian base being refueled and a Curtiss F8C that bears the early Squantum emblem on its fuselage. *(Courtesy of Peter B. Mersky)*

During a visit to Squantum in the late 1930s, a new Vought SB2U Vindicator dive-bomber and its crew pose for the local camera. Although touted as a highly capable combat aircraft, the SB2U's short wartime career was dismal. *(Courtesy of Peter B. Mersky)*

Following World War II, Squantum pilots and aircrews operated a variety of aircraft on training and proficiency missions. The SNJ, pictured here cloaked in the heavy snow of a New England winter, was one of the stalwart trainers flown at Squantum as well as elsewhere in the navy. *(Courtesy of Peter B. Mersky)*

Descended from NRAB Squantum, NAS South Weymouth is the only reserve base dedicated to aviation in the entire Northeast, including the six-state New England area. Blimps became a familiar sight along the East Coast after the commissioning of South Weymouth in 1952. The huge hangar not only housed the giant "gas bags," but also provided storm protection for other station aircraft. *(Courtesy of Peter B. Mersky)*

but its role in the development of the Naval Air Reserve and its position as the "first" Naval Air Reserve base have earned Squantum a special distinction in the history of the Naval Air Reserve.

NAS SOUTH WEYMOUTH

NAS South Weymouth had its origin during the era of the navy's lighter-than-air (LTA) program. In 1940, Captain Charles Rosendahl, chief of the navy's LTA program, was leading the fight for a base in the New England area. A 335-acre tract of land that took in small sections of Weymouth, Rockland, and Abington, Massachusetts, proved to be the most suitable and was chosen to be the site of a major navy lighter-than-air base. The U.S. Naval Air Facility, South Weymouth, Massachusetts, was commissioned 1 March 1942. (It was redesignated NAS in 1943.)

A huge blimp hangar was built early in 1942. Covering eight acres, it was the second-largest hangar in the world. This structure, which became a familiar landmark in the Boston South Shore area, was 956 feet long, 330 feet wide, and 191 feet high. The hangar could accommodate six of the ZPG-type blimps at one time. (During the 1954 hurricane season, every aircraft aboard the base, including the two blimps and much of the heavy automotive equipment, was stored within this hangar for protection against impending storms.)

Throughout World War II, blimps stationed at Weymouth lent their support to antisubmarine warfare by patrolling the waters off the Atlantic Coast. In June 1944, six blimps took off from South Weymouth to establish the first "blimp barrier" squadron at Port Lyautey, French Morocco, North Africa, for patrolling the Straits of Gibraltar.

Following World War II, NAS South Weymouth was placed in a caretaker status, but not for long. In December 1950, plans were begun to rebuild South Weymouth and make the base suitable for modern training

110

A "formation" of blimps over South Weymouth. The Naval Air Reserve established lighter-than-air squadrons at South Weymouth, Lakehurst, New Jersey, and Moffett Field, California.

Below During a 1954 hurricane, all of South Weymouth's aircraft and motor vehicles found shelter inside the giant blimp hangar, including two blimps.

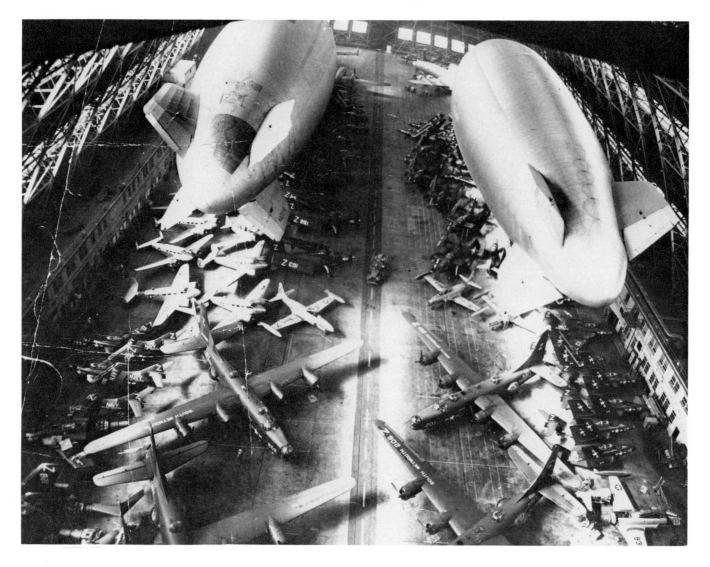

This 1989 view of NAS South Weymouth shows the north-south runway on the right, the east west runway and VP-92's flightline at the top. Marine A-4Ms are parked on the ramp in the right center of the photograph. *(Photo by PH1 David Meyer)*

of navy and marine reservists, then training at the soon-to-be-closed Squantum NRAB. In December 1953, U.S. Naval Air Station South Weymouth was recommissioned. Captain Harry Sartoris, USNR, the last commanding officer of NRAB Squantum, became the first CO of NAS South Weymouth. It was also Captain Sartoris who flew the last aircraft from Squantum to the new facility at South Weymouth.

With room to operate and expand, the reserve got on with the business of training and proficiency. Patrol, reconnaissance, and support squadrons were added to the air station in the sixties, although the most visible symbol of the station, the dirigibles, disappeared as the last blimp squadron was disestablished in 1961.

NAS South Weymouth continued to grow during the sixties and seventies as the navy's only reserve base in New England. Today, the base is host to forty reserve commands, including a P-3 squadron, an SH-2G LAMPS squadron, and marine A-4 and UH-1 squadrons.

ANACOSTIA

The Naval Air Reserve in Washington, D.C., was established in 1926. Lieutenant Edward Rounds, USNR, was tasked with organizing and recruiting a Naval Air Reserve squadron that would serve Washington, D.C., and its adjoining areas in Maryland and Virginia. The squadron was to be based at the Anacostia Naval Reserve Air Base, just across the Potomac River from what is today National Airport. The squadron was designated VT-30 Reserve Aviation Squadron and was assigned one Curtiss N2C. In 1930, two more N2Cs were assigned so that the squadron "had enough aircraft to fly formation." As with other NRABs in existence at this time, the primary role of Anacostia was the training and proficiency of reserve aviators. When World War II broke out, the men of Anacostia were integrated into the fleet, and Anacostia began primary flight training. Over 1,500 cadets were trained at Anacostia during the war.

After the war, Anacostia returned to its role as a reserve base, but it wasn't long until the regular navy looked to it again for help. When the Korean War required calling out selected units of the Naval Air Reserve, VP-661, flying PBYs, was activated on 20 July 1950. VP-661 was again activated to respond to the Berlin crisis in 1961, this time flying P2V aircraft.

In late 1961, the Anacostia aviation base was closed due to expanded air traffic at National Airport and a freeway skirting the field that limited its expansion. With the assignment of jet aircraft imminent, the Washington reserve forces were moved to nearby Andrews Air Force Base where the longer runways could accommodate the AF-1E Fury jets and the C-54 transports that would soon arrive in the reserve's fleet. NAF Washington is still an active reserve base, home to a P-3 antisubmarine squadron, an EA-6B electronic warfare squadron, and a transport squadron.

This early photo shows NRAB Anacostia soon after its establishment in 1926. Located at the junction of the Potomac and Anacostia rivers, NRAB Anacostia was an ideal site for the Naval Air Reserve in the nation's capital during the early years.

Reserve aircrewmen from Anacostia pose by one of their SB2C Helldivers during a drill weekend in 1950. Anacostia's runways were not long enough to accommodate the newer generation of aircraft that were replacing the Helldivers in the '50s, forcing the Naval Air Reserve to look for another home in the Washington, D.C., area.

An inspection in October 1932 had Anacostia's reserve aircraft in parade formation on the station's small ramp. A Ford JR Trimotor and other aircraft can be seen as well.

The pressures of postwar development, the need for longer runways to accommodate new aircraft, and air traffic growth at National Airport across the Potomac River forced the cessation of flight operations at Anacostia. The Naval Air Reserve moved to its new home, the east side of Andrews Air Force Base, in 1961. Patrol squadrons VP-661, 662, and 663, flying P2V Neptunes, were among the first tenants at the new Naval Air Facility, Washington, D.C.

NAF Washington in 1990. This aerial view of Andrews Air Force Base near Washington, D.C., shows the dual north-south runways. The air force complex, home of "Air Force One," is located at the top of the photo. At the bottom is the Naval Air Facility, on the east side of the base.

NEW YORK

Naval Air Reserve activity in the New York area dates back to the very beginning of air reserve history. A Naval Air Reserve unit was opened in Fort Hamilton, Brooklyn, around the same time that Trubee Davison formed the first Yale Unit. The unit moved to nearby NAS Rockaway in 1926 and then to Curtiss Field, Valley Stream, Long Island, in 1929. In 1928, the City of New York commissioned Clarence Chamberlin, a noted aviator, to study airports abroad and recommend to the city where to locate an airport. Chamberlin explored the New York area extensively and selected Barren Island in Jamaica Bay as the best location. New York City raised the swampy island to sixteen feet above sea level by pumping sand out of Jamaica Bay. The elevated 321-acre site was then connected to nearby Flatbush Avenue, a direct route to New York City.

The new field was named Floyd Bennett Municipal Airport. Rear Admiral Richard E. Byrd dedicated the field to the memory of his copilot who flew with him on the historic flight over the North Pole. Both Admiral Byrd and Warrant Officer Bennett received the Medal Of Honor for that flight. Bennett later died of pneumonia, contracted as a result of his gallant attempts to rescue three downed fliers whom he had never known.

On 1 April 1931, the Naval Air Reserve in New York moved to Hangar 5 at Floyd Bennett Municipal Field. The mission of the unit was to train reservists, recruit aviation cadets, and conduct "elimination" flight training to screen out candidates who were not aeronautically suitable for further training.

An aerial view of Floyd Bennett Field, Jamaica Bay, New York. This field had an illustrious history as a civil aviation airport prior to its conversion to a naval air station during World War II.

NAS New York reverted to the Naval Air Reserve Training Command after World War II. This F6F-5 Hellcat was typical of aircraft flown by Floyd Bennett reserve squadrons. (The R on the tail was the identifier for New York, not a designation as a reserve aircraft.) *(Courtesy of Roger Besecker)*

In the ten years following its dedication as a municipal airport, many aviation firsts were recorded at Floyd Bennett. Wiley Post flew his Lockheed Vega "Winnie Mae" around the world in seven days, nineteen hours, taking off and landing at Floyd Bennett Field. Jacqueline Cochran set a new transcontinental speed record of 234.7 mph in 1938, concluding her flight at Floyd Bennett Field. With the outbreak of war in 1941, however, all civilian flying ceased at Floyd Bennett as the country mobilized for war. The navy purchased the airfield from the City of New York for $9,500,000 and turned the airport into NAS New York.

During World War II NAS New York served as home station for antisub units, fleet service squadrons, cadet flight training, and the Ferry Command, which delivered aircraft from eastern factories to the fleet. In 1943 the NAS became a main terminal for MATS (Military Air Transport System) transcontinental flights.

Following the war, the air station resumed duties as a Naval Air Reserve training station. Units from NAS New York were mobilized for both the Korean War and the *Pueblo* crisis. The base was finally decommissioned in the early seventies, another victim of conflicting civilian air traffic and a lack of space.

SAN FRANCISCO BAY AREA

Like New York, the San Francisco Bay area has played a large role in reserve aviation history. In 1928 members of the first Bay Area Reserve Squadron rented a hangar and two seaplanes and established a unit at Naval Reserve Air Base, Oakland, California. Calling themselves the Golden Gaters, this colorful group led by Lieutenant Francis B. Connell, escorted Count Von Eckner over San Francisco Bay during his round-the-world trip in the Graf Zeppelin. The same unit also accompanied Amelia Earhart out to sea on her first round-the-world attempt.

During World War II, the reserve moved operations to Livermore, California, where they trained student aviators. Following the war, the

The Grumman JF-3 was a familiar sight in the San Francisco Bay area in the years before WW II.

Golden Gaters returned to Oakland, where they became a naval air station under the newly established chief of naval air reserve training. The NAS at Oakland was officially closed in 1961, ending one era of reserve history for San Francisco but beginning another. The three-thousand U.S. Navy and Marine Corp reservists moved operations to the naval air station at Alameda and continued the proud tradition of the Naval Air Reserve in San Francisco Bay, operating under the control of the Naval Air Reserve Training Unit, Alameda.

LOS ALAMITOS

Naval Reserve aviation in southern California started in 1928. Operating out of a barn-like hangar, one officer, one petty officer third-class yeoman, and one ancient but willing UO-1 aircraft—flown as fuel availability permitted—started a reserve presence in southern California that would eventually grow to thousands of men and women and hundreds of aircraft. The Naval Reserve Air Base on Cherry Street in Long Beach was established, as were many of the early naval reserve bases, as a result of the enthusiasm for naval aviation displayed by local citizen groups and the efforts of these groups to promote an aviation reserve program. In southern California, one name, Lieutenant Esten B. Koger, USNR, stands out as the influential naval officer who created ties with the city of Long Beach that enabled the Los Alamitos naval reserve air station to eventually become one of the largest and most active in the reserve establishment.

By 1937, the southern California Naval Air Reserve had progressed a long way since its humble beginnings. Flight operations had increased

The Naval Reserve Air Base at Long Beach. The long and proud history of the Naval Air Reserve in southern California began at Long Beach in 1928.

Los Alamitos as it appeared from the air in the late '60s shortly before it was closed. An enlarged version of this photograph was displayed in the operations building so pilots could avoid the ever-increasing number of noise-sensitive areas.

to a point where the military traffic was interfering with civilian traffic at Long Beach Airport, and the modest facilities at the original base were inadequate. The Naval Reserve Air Base moved to a new location off Spring Street that had two hangars, an overhaul building, and a new runway. Between these new facilities and the recently passed Aviation Cadet Program, applicants for the naval reserve flying program were waiting in line to join. The opportunity to learn to fly and serve their country must have been strong motivators for those early reservists. It certainly wasn't the pay. Five to fifteen dollars a month was the average drill pay in those days.

The reserve base in southern California was moved again shortly after World War II broke out. That outbreak resulted in a rapidly expanded pilot-training program, with the attendant need for more facilities such as barracks. The Spring Street location was simply inadequate. As a result, Los Alamitos Naval Air Station was commissioned in 1942 on 1,300 acres of land in a (then) unpopulated area of Long Beach. During the war, Los Alamitos served as a primary training base, using N3Ns and Piper Cubs to train hundreds of pilots for the war effort. The base also became an important air group staging center for aircraft deploying to the Pacific combat area.

The rapid expansion of flight training during WW II required more space than was available at the Long Beach NRAB. A new base at NAS Los Alamitos was established to accommodate the needed growth. Here, commissioning festivities take place in August 1942 when Los Alamitos was designated a naval air station.

A VF-781 Panther catches an arresting wire aboard the USS *Bonhomme Richard* following a mission over Korea. VF-781, a reserve squadron based at NAS Los Alamitos, volunteered en masse to go on active duty during the Korean War. *(Photo by John Woods)*

119

After the war, Los Alamitos remained active in reserve training. F6Fs, F4Us, PV-1s, and TBMs were common sights over Long Beach as the reorganized reserve created opportunities for World War II aviators to maintain their aviation skills if needed for future conflicts. They would be. When the Korean War broke out, six squadrons from Los Alamitos were activated, including VF-781, which volunteered to a man to go on active duty.

Los Alamitos squadrons again answered the bell during the Berlin crisis when VS-771 and VS-772 were called up, and during the *Pueblo* crisis in 1968 when VA-876 was selected for mobilization.

Unfortunately, Los Alamitos fell victim to the same fate that has befallen so many other Naval Air Reserve bases. Air-traffic congestion and urban growth around the airport combined with budget cuts to write the final chapter in the illustrious history of Naval Reserve Air bases in Long Beach. Control of Los Alamitos was turned over to the California Air National Guard in 1976, ending fifty years of reserve history in the Los Angeles area.

NAS TWIN CITIES

The Twin Cities of Minneapolis/St. Paul, Minnesota, are a long way from either the Atlantic or the Pacific Ocean, but this community's ties with the navy and the Naval Air Reserve go back to the beginning of naval aviation and transcend its land-locked location.

The relationship between the people of the upper Midwest and the navy can be traced back to World War I when the Dunwoody Naval Training School was established in Minneapolis on 31 July 1917. This school was one of three similar training institutions and was the only

The first squadron at NRAB Minneapolis: VN-11-RD9 (Reserve Training Squadron 11, Ninth Naval District).

An aerial view of NRAB Minneapolis during a change of command ceremony in the '30s.

Elimination training became a primary job for NRAB Minneapolis immediately before World War II. Here, aviation cadets line up in front of their N3N trainers.

The Curtiss series of dive-bombers served the fleet and reserve in the 1930s, and could be found in reserve units from Minneapolis to Long Beach. NRAB Minneapolis reservists stand in the mid-winter snow before starting their O2Cs.

one not located on a coast. The school trained over five thousand students in its two years before deactivation in 1919. The success of the school and the strong community support showed the navy that the upper Midwest made up for its lack of proximity to salt water with its enthusiasm for the navy. The groundwork had been laid for a long association between the two.

The Naval Air Reserve remembered the Twin Cities as it progressed from a fledgling status into a growing organization. As naval aviation training grew in the mid-'20s, several bases were established where elimination flight training was conducted. The Naval Reserve Air Base at Minneapolis was one. Located on the east side of the newly constructed civilian airport, Wold-Chamberlin Field, NRAB Minneapolis quickly established itself as one of the Naval Air Reserve's top bases. In 1931, this reputation was validated when NRAB Minneapolis received the highest mark awarded to any of the NRABs during their annual inspections.

By 1936 NRAB Minneapolis was one of the primary locations for the navy's elimination training program. Qualified candidates were given thirty-day tryouts, and if they passed this trial successfully, they were sent to Pensacola, Florida, for further training.

As the possibility of war loomed in the late thirties, the navy began a million-dollar construction program at Minneapolis. To facilitate this growth and expansion, further land was acquired from the Minneapolis Park Board for the air base. This expansion proved to be most timely when World War II broke out and the need for pilots mushroomed. The role of NRAB Minneapolis changed from elimination flight training to primary flight training. At the outbreak of war, the navy base at Twin Cities had 17 officers and 122 enlisted men attached to it. Slightly more than a year later, the station was training 436 cadets, and by May 1944, 3,579 persons were serving aboard the newly redesignated naval air station. By the end of the war, 4,232 cadets had been trained in the initial phases of flight instruction at Minneapolis. One of the 4,232 cadets who

The F4U Corsair became a primary postwar mount for the Naval Air Reserve. These F4Us were based at Minneapolis. *(Courtesy of Jim Sullivan)*

The Naval Air Reserve entered the jet age with such aircraft as the Grumman F9F Panther. These jets are from Minneapolis in the late '50s.

received his primary flight training at NAS Minneapolis was George Herbert Walker Bush.

Following World War II, NAS Minneapolis was placed under the control of the Chief of Naval Air Reserve Training. Its new mission was to retain experienced aviators in the Naval Air Reserve and to train them to maintain their flying skills, a role it performed for two decades.

NAS Minneapolis was renamed NAS Twin Cities on 3 July 1963. During the sixties, reservists based at Minneapolis flew attack, helicopter, transport, and patrol aircraft. Unfortunately, NAS Twin Cities fell victim to wide-sweeping budget cuts in the late '60s, and was closed during the summer of 1970. A Naval Air Reserve Detachment (renamed Naval Air Reserve Center Twin Cities in July 1979) remained at Minneapolis, maintaining the long and proud association between the Naval Air Reserve and the people of the upper Midwest.

NAS SEATTLE

The Naval Air Reserve in Seattle, Washington, began in 1925 with the establishment of the Naval Reserve Air Base, Sand Point. The air base was built on the site of a former golf course when that area was deemed the only location suitable for a landing field. On 8 March 1926, King County deeded the 400-acre site to the navy, creating one of the most scenic naval bases in the United States.

NRAB Seattle was used initially to conduct elimination flight training for prospective flight students and as a training facility for reserve pilots previously qualified. In 1929 it had the distinction of hosting the first Soviet aircraft to land in the United States. The base experienced major development in 1937 under the leadership of a new commanding officer, Lieutenant Commander Arthur Radford (who would later become a full admiral, chief of naval operations, and chairman of the Joint Chiefs of Staff). Three new hangars, a dispensary, a bachelor officers' quarters, a naval reserve building, administration building, and additions to storehouses were built during Lieutenant Commander Radford's tenure. The runway was also lengthened, making NAS Seatthe one of the best airfields in the Northwest. As a result of Lieutenant Commander Radford's initiative and foresight, NRAB Seattle was able to play a major role when World War II broke out.

From October 1942 until the end of the war, the station's facilities were used for forming and re-forming fleet combat squadrons as well as for the overhaul of aircraft engines and seaplanes. NAS Seattle (re-designated 1943) won a reputation as an efficient, comfortable, and hospitable base where war-weary aviators from the Aleutians, Pacific, and Philippines could re-form squadrons from fragmented units.

Early aircraft assigned to NRAB Seattle included an O2C.

With its newly lengthened runway and other base improvements, NRAB Seattle was able to play an important role when World War II broke out. Thousands of pilots were trained at the Northwest base.

Following the war, NAS Seattle came under the control of the newly organized Chief of Naval Air Reserve Training Command, and training and proficiency of reserve aviators became its primary role. The importance of this role was borne out as Seattle-based squadrons FASRON-895, VS-892, and VP-892 were called to active duty during the Korean conflict and VS-891 was mobilized during the Berlin crisis in 1961.

Squadron changes within the Naval Air Reserve Training Command to meet changing fleet needs also affected NAS Seattle in 1963, 1965, and 1966. The first change involved disestablishing VR-891 and VS-894 to augment the two remaining squadrons of their types on board. In 1965, attack squadrons 891 and 892 were also decommissioned, marking the final phase-out of A-1 aircraft in the reserve inventory.

Seattle was a victim of the same base-closings act that eliminated NAS Olathe and NAS Twin Cities in 1970. Reserve force squadrons were moved to Whidbey Island, and other units were dispersed to various reserve centers on the West Coast.

NAF DETROIT

The Naval Air Reserve in Detroit dates back to the 1920s. As early as 1925, four navy men with an interest in aviation were meeting in the Naval Armory on the shore of the Detroit River, near the site of the present-day Naval Armory. The next year, this unofficial organization was placed under navy administration and designated as a torpedo squadron, VT-31.

Initially, the navy flew its single aircraft from Selfridge Field, then run by the army. In 1928, the Michigan Naval Force, as it was known, moved to its own strip of land on an island in the Detroit River, known as Grosse Ile.

Two other aviation activities shared the southern end of the island in the late '20s. Curtiss-Wright Company and a dirigible company had built an aircraft hangar and a balloon hangar bordering the wide-open field adjacent to the naval base. In the early '30s, both companies closed down, so the state leased the land and buildings to the federal government for the Naval Reserve Air Base. There were no runways then except for a circular concrete country road around the field. It was used occasionally to taxi aircraft down to the seaplane base from the new headquarters in the Curtiss-Wright hangar.

During the '30s, the emphasis at Grosse Ile was on improvement and refinement of military aircraft and flying techniques. Few changes were made in the physical size and setup of the base. For the three to four squadrons that were based there, an officers' quarters and enlisted men's barracks were built side by side on the road that was then the northern boundary of the station.

World War II brought big expansion to Grosse Ile. The base almost doubled in size with the construction of a new, much-larger hangar, a large drill hall, wide concrete runways, and a huge center mat.

With the end of the war came a change in the station's mission. Instead of training pilots to go to war, the station now became a center for helping pilots and aviation specialists who had come home from the war to maintain their hard-earned and valuable experience. The air station became part of the nationwide Naval Air Reserve Training Command and host to thousands of "weekend warriors."

The introduction of jet aircraft into the Naval Air Reserve made longer runways necessary. Efforts to expand the runways at Grosse Ile for high-

A-4B Skyhawks from NAS Twin Cities during the late '60s. The jet squadrons were transferred to Detroit when Twin Cities NAS was closed.

performance jet operations were blocked, however, by the local township board. The navy had to transfer most fighter and attack pilots into squadrons at other stations, such as Minneapolis and Chicago. Transport, patrol, and helicopter crews continued training at Grosse Ile until 1969 when the navy decided to move thrity miles north to Selfridge Field, where navy aircraft had flown over forty years before.

Naval Air Facility Detroit, was established on 9 November 1969 on the west side of the airfield. It was the first tenant command established at Selfridge when control of the base was transferred from the air force to the Michigan Air National Guard. Today, the navy is the largest command located at Selfridge. Two reserve force squadrons call Selfridge home: VR-62 flying C-9Bs and VP-93 flying P-3s. Selfridge hosts over a thousand selected reservists drilling with various reinforcing and sustaining units. In addition, NAF Detroit is responsible for administering training at Naval Air Reserve Center Columbus, Ohio, where twelve additional units perform drills.

This A-1E was the largest aircraft to fly out of Grosse Ile. With the arrival of jets, the base was closed and Naval Air Reserve activities moved to nearby Selfridge Air Force Base. *(Photo by Ira Ward)*

The Naval Air Reserve in Detroit moved to Grosse Ile in 1930, taking over an aircraft hangar and a balloon hangar that had been abandoned.

This southerly view of Naval Air Facility Detroit shows the hangar complex and ramp facility at Selfridge Air Force Base, home to VP-93 and VR-62. *(Photo by W. W. Bollinger)*

NAS GLENVIEW

The Chicago, Illinois, area has been a vital part of the Naval Air Reserve history almost from its very beginning. In fact, the third Naval Reserve Air Base established was near Chicago at Great Lakes, Illinois. Initially, the reservists flew seaplanes from shore facilities at nearby Lake Michigan, and later, land planes from a small field on the Naval Training Station at Great Lakes.

The limited facilities of the Great Lakes Naval Station proved inadequate to accommodate the newer and larger aircraft that evolved in the thirties. Rear Admiral John Downes, USN, commandant of the Ninth Naval District, recommended that the NRAB be moved to the Curtiss-Reynolds Airport in Glenview, Ilinois, about ten miles southwest of Great Lakes. The recommendation was approved, and construction began on 4 January 1937.

The official dedication ceremonies for the base were held at 1500 on 28 August 1937, complete with a band playing and aircraft flight demonstrations. FF-2s, O2Cs, and OJs flew in from reserve bases at Chicago, Minneapolis, Kansas City, St. Louis, and Grosse Ile to participate. They demonstrated dive-bombing, strafing, the Luffbery Circle, and aerial combat. As one reporter put it, "The flying was of the highest caliber even though each division was made up of pilots from the other five reserve bases in the district who had no previous practice together."

N-3Ns over NAS Glenview in the early 1940s—Glenview expanded rapidly after the outbreak of World War II.

Glenview's role over the next three years was primarily elimination flight training for students seeking appointments as aviation cadets. Those students that met the required standards were transferred to NAS Pensacola for further training. In 1941, however, the United States's entry into World War II appeared imminent, and it was apparent to naval aviation leaders that the primary flight-training facilities concentrated at Pensacola, Florida, could not handle the expansion that would be required. Accordingly, navy planners decided to transfer primary flight training to naval reserve bases across the country and use Pensacola for advanced training. Due to Chicago's central location, it was decided that Glenview would be used as an experiment in the expansion of primary flight training. On 24 March 1942, Lieutenant Commander G.A.T. Washburn relieved Lieutenant Commander Gaines and directed the expansion of what was to become the largest primary training facility in naval aviation. An ambitious construction program was developed and a contract signed by April 7. In 121 working days, 1,300,000 square feet of concrete for taxiways, ramps, and runways were poured. New hangars and administration and training buildings were built. The construction program as originally planned was completed by late November 1942. On New Year's Day, 1943, NRAB Chicago was redesignated Naval Air Station Chicago, Glenview. In 1944, "Chicago" was deleted and the station became NAS Glenview.

The ambitious construction program paid dividends. Nearly 9,000 aviation cadets received their primary flight training at Glenview during

Four F9Fs from Glenview fly over Chicago in the late '50s. Noise problems and airspace congestion eventually resulted in the transfer of the jet squadrons to other reserve bases.

The Naval Air Reserve "Air Barons" perform during one of their airshows. This reserve flight demonstration team was in existence for only about five years, but during that time they thrilled crowds with their aerial skill and introduced the Naval Air Reserve to hundreds of thousands of people. The team flew A-4Bs initially, and transitioned to A-4Ls as seen above.

A P-3 from VP-60 flies over the modern Chicago skyline. Glenview is home to two patrol squadrons, VP-60 and VP-90.

130

World War II. This represented over 800,000 flight hours and more than two million takeoffs and landings.

In 1946 Glenview discontinued its role as a primary training base and became headquarters for the newly formed Naval Air Reserve Training Command. The role of this command was to establish reserve bases throughout the nation where experienced aviators from World War II could affiliate and maintain their aviation proficiency should their hard-won skills be needed for future conflicts.

Glenview has played an important role in reserve aviation ever since. Glenview squadrons were mobilized for the Korean War and the Berlin crisis. Glenview was the home of the Air Barons, the Naval Air Reserve flight demonstration team that performed impressively for five years between 1967 and 1972.

In 1973, the Naval Air Reserve Training Command became the Naval Air Reserve Force, and the headquarters moved to New Orleans to consolidate with the Naval Reserve Surface Force. NAS Glenview is still an important base in the Naval Air Reserve, however. Today, Glenview is home to two P-3 squadrons, VP-60 and VP-90, and a C-9 squadron, VR-51. Additionally, twenty-seven reinforcing/sustaining reserve units drill at Glenview, and the base is host to tenant commands from the army, coast guard, air force, and marines. NAS Glenview is now responsible for the management of Naval Air Reserve training programs at Naval Air Reserve Center, Twin Cities, Minnesota, where more than a dozen units perform drills.

NAS WILLOW GROVE

The Naval Air Reserve in Pennsylvania began at the Philadelphia Navy Yard in 1929. The unit, consisting of sixteen officers, fifty-three enlisted men, four seaplanes, and seven land planes, was transferred from the abandoned Rockaway, New York, training school. In Philadelphia, the unit set up their operations at Mustin Field on the grounds of the Philadelphia Navy Yard. This facility was the center of all reserve aviation in the entire naval district until the end of the '30s.

The Philadelphia reserve unit was initially designated as a primary flight-training unit, with emphasis on elimination training for cadets.

A-4 squadrons from Glenview during a carrier-qualification period.

The "Yellow Peril" was classroom to thousands of naval aviators in the years before and during World War II. Many versions of the famous trainer were manufactured, and a few of the originals have been restored like the one pictured here. *(Photo by A. Sparling)*

NAS Willow Grove was built on this site—Pitcairn Airfield—after the navy purchased the land in 1946.

When World War II broke out, however, the mission was changed to squadron operational training. The unit designed programs to mold groups of noncombat pilots and enlisted men into well-balanced fighting units through a syllabus of combat team tactics, gunnery, bombing, and rocket firing.

The expanded air operations spawned by the threat of war necessitated more room than was available at the Philadelphia Navy Yard. In 1941, the navy purchased the 576-acre Pitcairn Airfield located in northwestern Montgomery County, about seventeen miles from downtown Philadelphia. The airfield was named after its former owner, Harold Pitcairn, who was the inventor of the autogyro, predecessor to the helicopter.

In 1942 the first contingent of navy personnel arrived at their new home. This group consisted of 250 officers and enlisted men and an aircraft complement of thirty N3N "Yellow Peril" biplanes. In January

Willow Grove reservists flew these FH-1 Phantoms during the early '50s.

Squad members pose in front of their aircraft during annual active duty for reservists drilling at Willow Grove.

ASW has always been a big role for Willow Grove–based squadrons. These S-2 Trackers were assigned to Willow Grove in the '60s.

Lieutenant Chris Willy, a naval flight officer instructor at the Reserve Antisubmarine Training Center, explains system operation of the advanced P-3 tactical weapons systems to Ensign Joe Lyon from VP-68.

1943, Pitcairn Airfield was commissioned Naval Air Station, Horsham, renamed Naval Air Station, Willow Grove later in the same year. In 1957 the navy purchased additional acreage from bordering residents, giving the air station a total of 1,000 acres.

The same year, the Reserve Antisubmarine Warfare Training Center (RESASWTRACEN) was created. This school, initially called the Reserve Antisubmarine Warfare Tactical School, was established to provide operational and maintenance training for Naval Air Reserve personnel assigned to antisubmarine operations. The school possesses sophisticated trainers that enable ASW crews to train together as a team in sub-hunting exercises. In 1981, RESASWTRACEN became a separate command with an expanded mission to provide ASW training for naval reserve, active-duty, and foreign military personnel. It also has become the center of P-3 standardization for all crew members. The school is the only one of its kind.

Willow Grove is home base for two P-3B reserve force squadrons, VP-64 and -66. VR-52, a C-9B squadron, and HSL-94, an SH-2G LAMPS ASW squadron, are also based at Willow Grove.

ST. LOUIS

The Naval Air Reserve in St. Louis goes back to 1925 when a Naval Reserve Air Base was established under the command of Lieutenant (j.g.) Fred Fisher, USNR. The primary mission of the base was flight training during the '30s, a role that greatly increased during World War II, including the training of British cadets. St. Louis was one of the sites recommended by the Mason Board for expansion during the war years. (See below.)

In 1943, in keeping with its increased activity, NRAB St. Louis was redesignated NAS St. Louis. In late 1944, however, all flight training ceased, with the British cadets in training being transferred to NAS

133

Reserve aviators coming out of WW II and Korea were an experienced group, but accidents can happen even to veteran aviators. This F8F, assigned to NAS St. Louis, made a wheels-up landing at Goodfellow Air Force Base while on a cross-country training flight. The Naval Air Reserve had a significant presence in St. Louis until the base was closed in 1958. *(Courtesy of Fred Roos via Jim Sullivan)*

Bunker Hill, Indiana, and the American students to NAS Glenview. NAS St. Louis was transferred from the Training Command to the Ninth Naval District and became a base for ferry operations conducted by Ferry Service Three.

NAS St. Louis saw a big reduction in operations and personnel following the war. In 1946, however, control of NAS St. Louis was turned over to the Chief of Naval Air Reserve Training, and the mission changed to "support and provide facilities for Naval Air Reserve Training as directed by the Chief of Naval Air Reserve Training." Operations increased at NAS St. Louis as reservists affiliated in increasing numbers and aircraft squadrons grew.

Like so many bases, however, budget cuts and conflicts between civilian and military aviation doomed the Naval Air Reserve in St. Louis. The Naval Air Station was based aboard Lambert Field, the civilian airport for St. Louis, and the general mood of the city was to remove the military aircraft to relieve congestion. NAS St. Louis was disestablished on 31 January 1958.

THE MASON BOARD

As the threat of war grew in the late '30s, the navy realized that it had to expand its cadet training facilities significantly in order to train the many naval aviators that would surely be needed if war broke out. During the summer of 1940, a board of naval officers under Captain Charles F. Mason (thereafter known as the Mason Board) toured the country looking over sites for Naval Reserve Air Bases to train cadets. As might be expected, city officials were anxious for the revenue and jobs that a naval base would bring, so the members of the Mason Board were wined and dined at every stop. Perhaps the "arduous" nature of this duty caused the Mason Board to look at as many cities as it did, but the end result was a comprehensive study of possible cities across the United States. Based on the study, the board made its final recommendations in the following order of priority:

New Orleans	Columbus	Cleveland	Pittsburgh
Dallas	Buffalo	Memphis	Macon
Atlanta	Houston	Indianapolis	Albany
Denver	Birmingham	Cincinnati	Cheyenne
Nashville	Salt Lake City	Portland	Fort Worth

Olathe-based fighter squadron 774, flying F4Us, was recalled to active duty for two years during the Korean War. The "Bitter Birds" made a big name for themselves in this conflict. *(Courtesy of John A. Nave)*

The board also recommended the expansion of Philadelphia, Squantum, Anacostia, Seattle, Oakland, Long Beach, Grosse Ile, Glenview, Minneapolis, and St. Louis.

The navy went along with the Mason Board recommendations and set about to build three new air stations. New Orleans, Atlanta, and Dallas were built at the same time and were identical. Their facilities included a steel hangar, barracks for one hundred cadets, and gasoline storage for 50,000 gallons. The navy also followed through on the board's recommendation to expand several of the NRABs, specifically Minneapolis, St. Louis, Squantum, Seattle, and Glenview.

NAS OLATHE, KANSAS

The Naval Air Reserve in Kansas began at the Fairfax Airport in Kansas City. An executive with Trans World Airlines (TWA), Captain D. W. Tomlinson, USNR, was influential in establishing a Naval Air Reserve presence in Kansas. Captain Tomlinson, a former commanding officer of a Naval Air Reserve squadron at Floyd Bennett Field (NAS New York), was transferred from TWA headquarters in New York to Kansas City. Captain Tomlinson desired to continue his association with the Naval Air Reserve, and he was aware of numerous navy-trained pilots flying for TWA out of Kansas City who were ready and willing to join an organized reserve. Working with his boss at TWA, Jack Frye (a former naval aviator himself), Captain Tomlinson enlisted support from the Kansas City community and the Navy Department to establish a reserve base at Kansas City. His efforts were successful, and in the fall of 1935, a Naval Reserve Air Base was established at the Kansas City Municipal Airport. The mission of the base was primary flight training and maintenance of flight proficiency for naval reserve aviators in the Kansas City area.

The Municipal Airport proved to be less than ideal for primary flight training. The increasing air traffic in Kansas City and the prevalence of fog coming off the Kansas and Missouri rivers led Captain Tomlinson to search for an alternate location for a Naval Reserve Air Base as the 1930s ended. He was aware of an emergency field used by TWA near Olathe, Kansas. The area was usually free of fog and away from the air traffic of Kansas City. He recommended to the Navy Department that a base be built at Olathe and the Naval Reserve Air base at Kansas City be transferred there. With the threat of World War II growing, the navy agreed, and land was purchased for construction in 1939.

Bulldozed out of the prairie a thousand miles away from the nearest salt water, Naval Air Station Olathe was officially established under the command of Captain D. W. Tomlinson, USNR, on 1 October 1942. The basic plan for Olathe was to accommodate 1,000 students at one time as well as to provide service and maintenance for the fast-growing Naval Air Transport Service, which was flying a constant stream of aircraft from coast to coast with war materials.

Soon the Kansas skies were filled with Yellow Perils (N2S, N3N, NP, and N5S) as flight training swung into full gear. The original plan for

A view of the Olathe tower with a Douglas F4D Skyray on the flight line. A jet-transition unit was established at Olathe in the early fifties to train pilots in jet aircraft. *(Courtesy of AMCS Donald F. Pitts)*

Rear Admiral Fowler, Chief of Naval Air Reserve (right), stands by the last F4D during ceremonies at Olathe in 1966 celebrating the retirement of the Skyray. Admiral Fowler died in a house fire soon after this photo was taken. *(Courtesy of Nick Williams and Don Pitts)*

student numbers proved to be highly flexible as training demands changed. Eventually, over 4,500 students checked into Olathe for primary training.

In May 1943, a Kansas tornado destroyed over one hundred aircraft. Before the station could recover the loss, the mission of NAS Olathe was changed. VR-3, with transport aircraft procured from TWA, was established at NAS Olathe, and the Kansas Air Station became the headquarters for the Naval Air Transport Service.

After the war, the transport squadrons were transferred, and NAS Olathe was used for reserve training and proficiency. During the Korean War, Olathe-based Fighter Squadron 774 was recalled to active duty for two years. The Bitter Birds of VF-774 played a big role in that war. They saw six months of action aboard the USS *Boxer*, and their pilots averaged sixty-two missions each.

Olathe's runways were lengthened in 1951 to accept the first jets, the FJ-1s that appeared that year. A jet-training transition unit (JTTU) was established in 1954 that assisted propeller-trained pilots in transitioning to jet aircraft.

For two decades, reservists from the Midwest maintained their readiness and proficiency drilling with squadrons at NAS Olathe. The same budget cutback that caused NAS Twin Cities to close also resulted in the closing of Olathe. The base was closed in July 1970 with the understanding that the navy could retain thirteen buildings for nonflying reserve programs and the base would be available for mobilization. Many units were transferred to Memphis, Denver, and Dallas. Naval Air Reserve Center Olathe was established soon thereafter.

NAS ATLANTA

The Naval Air Reserve in Atlanta started out in 1940 at the site of the old Camp Gordon, a World War I training center seven miles east of Stone Mountain in Chamblee, Georgia. Construction started at NAS Chamblee and personnel began arriving in October 1940. Five months after the

Cartoon characters were drawn to convey the determination of America at war. Disney's famous Donald Duck became the feature figure for NRAB Atlanta's emblem before it became NAS Atlanta.

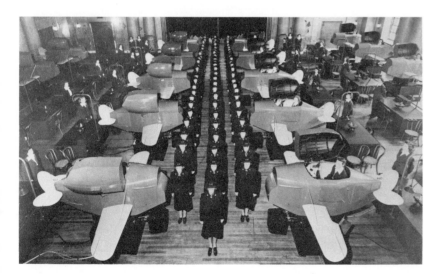

Line-up of Link trainers during World War II with their WAVE operators. NAS Atlanta was one of three reserve air stations established specifically to meet the demands of wartime pilot training.

SNJs fly in formation in this 1944 photo. Thousands of cadets underwent flight training at NAS Atlanta.

NAS Atlanta in the mid-eighties. The Naval Air Reserve shares the runway with the U.S. Air Force at Dobbins AFB.

station was commissioned, the first class of primary flight students began training on dirt runways. Thousands of cadets received training here throughout the war, as they did at the many Naval Reserve Air Bases that sprung up during the war years.

NAS Chamblee came under the control of the Naval Air Reserve Training Command in 1946, and its mission became the training of naval air reservists. As high-performance aircraft started making their way into the reserve fleet, the runways at the old site were no longer adequate. The Naval Air Reserve moved to the northwest section of Atlanta on 18 April 1959 on an airport shared with the air force and Lockheed Corporation. The base was renamed NAS Marietta, and later, NAS Atlanta.

NAS Atlanta has played an important role in the training and proficiency of naval air reservists ever since. F-9s, FJ-4s, F-8s, P-2s, and S-2s flew from NAS Atlanta during the sixties. After the reorganization in 1970, VA-205 was established as an attack squadron assigned to Reserve Carrier Air Wing Twenty. Transport squadron VR-46 had the distinction of being

Postwar naval air reservists check the flight board. After the war, NAS Atlanta reverted to a proficiency and training role for already-designated aviators.

A variety of trainers, including these N3Ns from the original Lake Pontchartrain base plied the skies over New Orleans on a regular basis in the '40s and '50s. The new facility at Belle Chase was completed in 1957, and the Naval Air Reserve began operations there the next year. Today, facilities at NAS New Orleans are shared by the Coast Guard, Marines, Air Force, and Army National Guard, as well as U.S. Customs.

The Naval Air Reserve at New Orleans started on the shores of Lake Pontchartrain during World War II.

the last squadron in the navy to fly the venerable C-118. Today VA-205 is transitioning from A-7Es to A-6Es, and VR-46 flies C-9s from NAS Atlanta. Additionally, the base provides support for a marine helicopter squadron and approximately twenty other reinforcing and sustaining units of the Naval Air Reserve.

NAS NEW ORLEANS

Naval aviation came to New Orleans in July 1941 as the threat of war grew. A Naval Reserve Air Base was established on the shores of Lake Pontchartrain, and was officially commissioned a naval air station in November 1942. The mission of NAS New Orleans was primary flight training for student naval aviators.

As with most reserve air bases, NAS New Orleans changed its mission after World War II and became responsible for training naval air reservists. In 1948, the idea of a joint air reserve center was conceived and plans laid for what is now NAS New Orleans. Congressman F. Edward Hebert was the dominating figure behind the establishment of a Joint Air Reserve Center. Construction of the field began in 1955, and in the fall of 1957 the first contingent of naval personnel was assigned to work stations. The station was opened in December 1957, and on 6 January 1958, the first Naval Air Reserve aircraft began operations. The field was dedicated in 1958 to Alvin Callender, a native of New Orleans, who lost his life in World War I while fighting with the Royal Flying Corps.

Today, thirty reinforcing/sustaining units and three reserve force

Reserve mechanics work on a TBM at the old NAS New Orleans.

squadrons (VP-94, VA-204, and VR-54) call Callender Field home. In addition to the Naval Air Reserve, Callender Field is home to the U.S. Air Force Reserve, the U.S. Marine Corps Reserve, the Louisiana Air National Guard, the U.S. Customs Service, and the U.S. Coast Guard. NAS New Orleans is unique in that all services have reserve air components there, making it the busiest of the reserve naval air stations.

NAS DALLAS

In October 1940 ground was broken for a Naval Reserve Air Base at a location midway between Dallas and Fort Worth near the town of Grand Prairie. The 319-acre plot was purchased by the city of Dallas and leased to the government for one dollar a year. A $2,000,000 contract was let for the construction of runways and necessary buildings, and the navy in Dallas—known locally as "The Prairie Navy"—was under way.

The base was officially commissioned on 15 May 1941. The total complement of the base consisted of 15 officers, 109 enlisted men, 35 flight students, and six Spartan training planes. The original mission of the station was to provide primary training for naval aviators. A secondary mission evolved from its co-location with the North American Aviation Plant (later LTV). NRAB Dallas was tasked to test and accept all aircraft delivered to the navy by the North American Aviation Plant. During the four years following its establishment, Dallas tested and accepted 4,421 SNJ Texan aircraft for the navy.

On 1 January 1943 the designation of the station was changed from NRAB to NAS Dallas. By then fifteen outlying fields were in use to accommodate the heavy training program. An auxiliary field, Lou Foote Field, now Grand Prairie Airport, was established to house Training Squadron Two and relieve congestion at the main station.

NAS Dallas was then tasked with a third function: the training of enlisted personnel in aviation skills for the navy, coast guard, and some foreign nationals. A contingent of Free French Forces arrived in 1943 to

An aerial photo of NAS Dallas in 1943. Dallas was commissioned in May 1941.

141

begin flight training. Of the eighteen French students who comprised the first class, thirteen had been awarded the croix de guerre for heroism at Dunkirk.

After the war, NAS Dallas reverted to the Naval Air Reserve. In September 1948 a Dallas reserve squadron made the first postwar training cruise by a reserve squadron, climaxed by carrier landings aboard the USS *Wright* off Pensacola, Florida.

Two years later, the same squadron, VA-702, responded to a more serious challenge by becoming the first reserve squadron to be recalled to active duty for a national emergency, in this case the Korean War. All together, six Dallas-based squadrons saw action in Korea.

NAS Dallas has seen its share of historic aircraft. Its squadrons flew the F6F during the Korean War and the FH-1 Phantom I in the early fifties. The swept-wing F9F Cougars and FJ Furies replaced Phantoms in 1954 through 1958. Also in 1958, E-14 arresting gear, employing a water-squeeze principle, was installed on the main runway. This was the first such gear to be used at a reserve air station. Another arresting gear first was scored by NAS Dallas in 1962 when the main runway was closed for repair. A mobile arresting gear unit, the first ever at a Naval Reserve Air Base, was installed so that operations could be conducted on Dallas's second runway, only 5,200 feet long.

In 1963, NAS Dallas became the first Naval Reserve Air Base to receive the supersonic F-8 Crusader. This venerable fighter was in service for thirteen years until replaced by the F-4N. Dallas's two fighter squadrons, VF-201 and 202, would later transition to the F-14.

Following the reserve reorganization in 1970, ASW warfare was phased out of NAS Dallas and the antisubmarine aircraft transferred to other stations. NAS Dallas retained the fighter squadrons and a transport squadron, VR-59.

In addition to its fighter and transport squadrons, NAS Dallas hosts the Fleet Logistic Support Wing and oversees training for more than thirty reinforcing/sustaining units. Other services maintain facilities at NAS Dallas, including the National Guard, the U.S. Army Reserve, the Texas Air National Guard, and Marine Air Group 41 flying the F-4S and CH-53A. Due to its convenient location for cross-country flights, it is one of the busiest small air stations. NAS Dallas is also responsible for training programs in the Rocky Mountain region where fifteen sustaining units drill at Buckley Air National Guard Base, home of Naval Air Reserve Center, Denver, Colorado.

NAS Dallas was the first reserve air station to fly the supersonic F-8 Crusader. The base is co-located with the LTV factory that manufactured the plane.

NAS Dallas is home today to VR-59 and two CVWR-20 F-14 fighter squadrons, VF-201 and VF-202. The facility is also shared with the Texas Air National Guard.

An aerial view of NAS Dallas today shows the southerly extension of the runway.

The shore station quarterdeck is a functional symbol of the seafaring heritage of naval aviation. Naval Air Reserve Center, Denver maintains the nautical tradition in the entrance to the facility's main training building.

OTHER AIR STATIONS

Following the war, new reserve naval air stations sprung up all over the country. The Chief of Naval Air Reserve Training wanted drilling sites located throughout the nation to make affiliation with the Naval Air Reserve easy for the thousands of naval aviators who had left active duty and relocated throughout the nation. Having bases accessible to the reservists' homes was essential for widespread participation in the new and expanding Naval Air Reserve.

With this objective in mind, naval air stations or facilities were established at Akron, Ohio; Birmingham, Alabama; Columbus, Ohio; Denver, Colorado; Houston, Texas; Lincoln, Nebraska; Niagara Falls, New York; and Spokane, Washington. These were in addition to the Naval Air Reserve Training Units that were established on already existing active-duty bases and the other reserve naval air stations that were transferred to the Chief of Naval Reserve Training following the war.

Most of these bases had relatively short histories. They succeeded in

144

making reserve affiliation and participation easier for reservists across the country and served their communities well, but most fell victim to the budget cutting that inevitably occurs when memories of war fade. Some of these bases are discussed below while table 8–1 (p. 159) displays a comprehensive list of reserve bases and their years of operation.

NAS Lincoln, Nebraska

NAS Lincoln was typical of the new bases that sprung up after the war. The base was located on Lincoln's municipal airfield, and its buildings consisted of abandoned army facilities vacated after World War II. Commander L. S. Melsom and his initial staff of three officers reported aboard in November 1948 with the responsibility of recruiting personnel and transforming the facility into an operational naval air station.

Commander Melsom and his crew wasted no time hiring civilians and enlisting stationkeeper personnel to begin the project. NAS Lincoln was officially commissioned on 15 December 1948, although it would be another year before the base received its first aircraft, an SNB ferried in from Spokane. Two months later the station received its first service-type aircraft—two F6F Hellcat fighters. In April of 1949, the Organized Reserve Air Group CVEG-85 was commissioned with a total count of forty-one officers, including thirty-two pilots, and eighty-nine enlisted men. CVEG-85 was commanded by Lieutenant Commander James Seybert, a World War II veteran who held three Air Medals and had downed six Japanese airplanes.

The base continued to grow in the early fifties, including the addition of a marine air reserve squadron, VMF-113. By 1958, a total of 613 reservists in seven squadrons and an air wing staff were drilling at NAS Lincoln. Unfortunately, "limited operating funds, increased costs of new aircraft and the reduction of personnel throughout the Navy" conspired to result in the closure of NAS Lincoln in February 1958.

Short-lived but still crucial to the mission of naval aviation in the '40s and '50s were a variety of small bases that grew up across the United States. This F9F-6 was from NAS Lincoln, Nebraska, where both active-duty and reserve aviators trained. *(Photo by Bill Larkins courtesy of Jim Sullivan)*

NAS Birmingham is little known and all but for-gotten in the archives of naval aviation. This Korean War–era photograph shows two McDonnell F2H Banshees, one a reserve aircraft and the other a photo version, over the USS *Kearsarge*.

NAS Akron

Naval aviation in Akron actually dated back to the earlier days when a school of instruction for kite balloons and dirigibles was established at Goodyear Field. The base was closed in 1920, however, and lay dormant until 1947 when NAS Akron was established as part of the Chief of Naval Air Reserve Training Command. In 1948 the mission of the base was expanded to provide support for a national stockpile of strategic and critical materials. For the next ten years, NAS Akron provided facilities to support navy and marine reserve flight training, having both lighter-than-air and heavier-than-air squadrons. NAS Akron was disestablished on 1 February 1958.

NAS Denver

Naval Air Station, Denver, Colorado, was established on 1 December 1946 with the primary mission of "providing facilities and support for Naval Air Reserve Training." NAS Denver was disestablished on 30 June 1959 along with the Naval Air Reserve Facility, Miami, Florida, the U.S. Naval Air Station, Columbus, Ohio, and the U.S. Naval Air Station, Niagara Falls, New York.

The F4U was probably the most manufactured aircraft in the history of naval aviation. Over 12,700 were built. They became the primary fighter aircraft of the navy after WW II and were operated from a variety of remote bases. The last delivery of the famous Corsair was made in January 1953. The aircraft above bear markings of bases at Birmingham, Miami, Niagara Falls, and Oakland. *(Photos courtesy of Jim Sullivan)*

NAS Niagara Falls

Niagara Falls had a modest beginning. With striking similarity to the early years of the Naval Air Reserve, reserve aviation came to Niagara Falls as a result of the hard work and dedication of a group of local citizens who were former naval aviators and wanted a Naval Air Reserve presence in their area. This group, wanting to maintain the hard-won skills they had gained during World War II, worked diligently and without pay to establish a Naval Air Reserve presence in the Buffalo, New York, area. In August 1947, this hard—and unpaid for—work paid off as the volunteers received permission from the navy to establish a Naval Air Reserve unit at Niagara Falls Airport. The unit was designated Aviation Volunteer Unit "A" and operated out of two wooden hangars used during World War II by Bell Aircraft.

The naval aviation group met twice a month without pay. Flying planes borrowed and flown to Niagara Falls from the Floyd Bennett Naval Air Station near Brooklyn, New York, the unit grew beyond the hopes of even the most optimistic. It soon became more and more difficult for the Brooklyn base to supply the growing Niagara unit with the necessary number of aircraft.

When reports of the unit's rapid growth reached naval headquarters, navy officials authorized expansion of the squadron to encompass the title of full-fledged naval air station. On 18 December 1948, The Niagara

Falls Naval Air Station was officially commissioned as a proud member of the nationwide Naval Air Reserve Training Command after sixteen months of existence as a volunteer unit. Units at Niagara Falls flew the F4U, the T2V jet trainer, the P2V Neptune, and the F2H-2 Banshee.

Despite the enthusiasm, motivation, and dedication of the naval aviation reservists at Niagara Falls, the base fell victim to budget cuts and was disestablished in June 1959.

NAVAL AIR RESERVE TRAINING UNITS

Following World War II, Naval Air Reserve Training Units (NARTUs) were created at many active-duty bases as part of the Chief of Naval Air Reserve Training's program to establish a reserve presence throughout the United States. By establishing reserve units on active-duty bases, many new drilling opportunities opened up beyond those available at the reserve naval air stations.

The primary role of the NARTUs was the same as reserve units everywhere: to retain valuable aviators in the Naval Air Reserve and keep them trained for mobilization. The NARTUs also played an important role in recruiting aviation candidates and telling the story of naval aviation to the communities where they were located. NARTUs were redesignated Naval Air Reserve Units in the seventies and later simply Naval Air Reserve, but their functions have remained similar.

NARTU Jacksonville

NARTU Jax was organized in April 1946 at Cecil Field Naval Auxiliary Air Station (now NAS Cecil). The command moved to nearby Jacksonville Naval Air Station shortly thereafter where it has been ever since. Experienced aviators from World War II affiliated with fighter and patrol

Atlanta reservists pose for a unique group photo on the wing of a P2V.

The unsung heroes of the Naval Air Reserve past and present are the recruiters whose job it is to assure that authorized program billets are filled by qualified, experienced personnel. Navy blimps, with decreasing operational commitments after WW II, were pressed into service as platforms for conspicuous advertisements.

NARTU Jax reserve aircraft of the '60s are grouped in front of the maintenance hangar.

squadrons at NARTU Jax, and the navy was soon reaping benefits. Fighter Squadron 741 and Patrol Squadron 741 were mobilized for active duty during the Korean War. Patrol Squadron 741 was again mobilized in 1961 to provide antisubmarine support for the fleet during the Berlin crisis.

NARTU Jax squadrons operated antisubmarine aircraft, patrol planes, trainers, transports, and jet attack aircraft throughout the sixties. Following the reorganization of the reserve in 1970, NARTU Jax relinquished control of the aircraft but still played a large role in the naval reserve organization. Today NAVAIRES Jacksonville provides services to Commander, Carrier Air Wing Reserve 20 located at Cecil Field. Aircraft from HS-75 and VP-62 fly from NAS Jacksonville.

The huge Lakehurst blimp hangars could be seen for miles and were a familiar landmark. NARTU Lakehurst's first reservists were lighter-than-air (LTA) pilots and ground crew. This undated photo, probably from the mid to late '40s, shows a Lakehurst blimp over NAS Squantum.

NARTU Lakehurst

The Naval Air Reserve Training Unit at NAS Lakehurst, New Jersey, was established in June 1947. The first naval air reservists attached to the unit were "lighter-than-air" (blimp) pilots. Many had hunted Hitler's U-boats during the battle of the Atlantic. The newly formed squadron ZP-751 soon attained the competence and level of operational efficiency that comes only with experienced pilots, always a hallmark of the Naval Air Reserve.

NARTU Lakehurst received its first fixed-wing Naval Air Reserve squadron in July 1954 when VS-751, flying the S-2F Tracker, checked aboard. The diversification of NARTU Lakehurst's squadrons continued the following year as Reserve Helicopter Utility Squadron (HU)-751 was formed. Its mission was air/sea rescue, ASW warfare, and harbor-patrol training.

Three more S-2 squadrons and one more HU squadron were assigned to Lakehurst by the end of the fifties, almost overshadowing the nostalgic decommissioning of the blimp squadron. Transport squadrons came to Lakehurst in the sixties, flying the C-117D, and later, C-54Q aircraft. VR-752 was one of the few Naval Air Reserve squadrons to participate in the Vietnam War, flying cargo to Vietnam during the squadron's two weeks of active duty in 1966.

A key element of the Naval Air Reserve has always been interaction with the local communities. The Naval Air Reserve at Lakehurst had one of the most successful community relations programs with its sponsorship of the New Jersey indoor track meet. Held at one of the cavernous old blimp hangars, the indoor track meet became an important event in the New Jersey high school track season. The track meet was held annually, and fostered much good will toward the Naval Air Reserve.

In 1970, Lakehurst became home to the newly formed Reserve Carrier Air Anti-Submarine Group 70, formed as a result of the post-*Pueblo* reorganization. Unfortunately, the periodic budget reviews and cutbacks that affected so many other reserve facilities befell the NARTU at Lakehurst in the mid-seventies. In 1976 the NARTU was disestablished, and a Naval Air Reserve Detachment under the control of NAS Willow Grove became the only reserve presence at NAS Lakehurst.

NARTU Norfolk

NARTU Norfolk was established on 1 July 1946. With a complement of thirty-five men and only a handful of aircraft, the Naval Air Reserve in Virginia started slowly but rapidly accelerated. The initial complement

Curtiss fighters line up with their crews in front of a hangar at NAS Norfolk. Naval aviation began in Hampton Roads, and it was natural that with the large fleet presence there a major reserve component would also flourish.

PV-2 Harpoon flight crews on the Norfolk flight line in the late '40s.

of obsolete aircraft eventually was replaced by the F8F Bearcat, PV Ventura, F4U-4 Corsair, FH1 Phantom, and the TBM Avenger. As the sixties evolved, the flight line at Norfolk included A-4Bs, S-2s, SH-34Js, C-54s, and several other utility aircraft.

A milestone in reserve aviation occurred in July 1964 when members of NARTU Norfolk's jet attack squadron (VA[J]-861) carrier-qualified aboard the USS *Lexington* in the Gulf of Mexico. These carrier qualifications in the A-4B Skyhawk were the first jet landings by reservists since the Korean War.

NARTU Norfolk was especially effective in generating goodwill for the navy and the Naval Air Reserve. It sponsored local soap-box derby contestants, a Little League baseball team, and encouraged members of the Norfolk community to visit the reserve facility and tour a special F-111 aircraft they had on display. Similar civic-minded activities went on at all NARTUs and promoted the civilian/sailor concept that is a critical part of the Naval Air Reserve.

NARTU Memphis

As with the other NARTUs, Memphis officially began operating on 1 July 1946. The primary mission of the unit was to provide training, support, and coordination for naval reservists who drilled and flew with the fighter, patrol, and transport squadrons based as NAS Memphis.

By mid-1948, two FH-1 Phantoms, were assigned to the reserves at Memphis. It was the venerable F4U, however, that saw action as Memphis-based Fighter Squadron 791 was recalled to active duty during the Korean War. Commander James B. Kisner led his squadron, VF-791, to Korea after mobilization in July 1950. The "Mid-South Rebels" flew off the USS *Boxer* for seven months without losing a single squadron member. The rebel flag became the insignia the squadron used for the rest of the war. NARTU Memphis provided another squadron, VP-793, during the Berlin mobilization.

NARTU Memphis also played an important recruit-training role in the sixties and early seventies. NARTU conducted recruit training for accelerated aircrew trainees from the entire Naval Air Reserve Training Command. The recruit received twenty-eight days of basic training and was then assigned to five months of rate training in specialties such as powerplants or electronics. At the end of the six months' active duty, the trainee was assigned to drill status with a reserve aviation squadron for practical training as an aircrewman.

In the mid-sixties NARTU Memphis was home to two A-4 attack squadrons, two P-2 patrol squadrons, and two VR squadrons flying C-54s. Following the reorganization of 1970, three reserve force squadrons—VA-204 (A-4s), VP-67 (P-2Es), VR-67 (C-118s)—were established at Memphis. The attack squadron moved to NAS New Orleans in 1978, but VR-60

Like many reserve bases, Memphis combined its resources to serve both naval and marine air reserve programs. Here a group of Tennessee marine reservists inspect an AF-1E Fury in 1966. *(Courtesy of Peter B. Mersky)*

NAS Memphis, Tennessee, is a familiar base to many naval aviators and maintenance specialists because of the extensive technical training mission of the base. Numerous squadrons and units have been assigned to the reserve command over the years. VF-791 made the point with this early fifties photograph.

A KA-3B takes off from NAS Alameda in this 1989 photo taken just before the "Whales" were retired from service. NARTU—and now NAVAIRES—Alameda has been home to many reserve squadrons and aviation support programs since the early '60s.

and VP-67 remain at Memphis, flying C-9Bs and P-3Bs, respectively. Memphis is also host to nearly 1,500 reservists drilling with fifteen reinforcing/sustaining units. In addition, NAVAIRES Memphis oversees and administers the training programs at the Naval Air Reserve Center, Olathe, Kansas.

NARTU Alameda, California

NARTU Alameda was established in March of 1961 following the closure of Naval Reserve Air Station Oakland, which was located a few miles south of the naval air station on the East Bay. At that time NARTU Alameda was the nation's second largest reserve aviation training facility and was host to 3,000 navy and Marine Corps reservists, 38 Naval Air Reserve squadrons and 32 other units.

In 1968, VA-873, an Alameda-based A-4B squadron, was recalled to active duty during the *Pueblo* crisis. After the *Pueblo* call-up, the Naval Air Reserve was reorganized, but Alameda continued to play a big role. The base was home to two A-7 attack squadrons, VA-303 and VA-304, and the only two A-3 refueling squadrons in the Naval Air Reserve. Many different types of naval aircraft have been assigned to Alameda reserve squadrons, but perhaps the base is best known as home to these reserve A-3s. Both VAK-208 and -308 flew the tanker version of the famous Skywarrior from NAS Alameda for nearly twenty years until they were retired from service in 1989.

NAVAIRES Alameda (redesignated "Naval Air Reserve Unit Alameda" in 1972 and simply "Naval Air Reserve Alameda" in 1983) today oversees

Other Oakland reserve aircraft included the F2H McDonnell Banshee, a successful second-generation jet fighter, and the Piasecki HUP helicopter that enjoyed a measure of success as a plane guard in the fleet. *(Courtesy of Peter B. Mersky)*

one of the largest concentrations of Naval Air Reserve programs on the West Coast. Four reserve squadrons—VA-304, VR-55, HS-85, and HM-19—three reinforcing units, and twenty-three sustaining units are located there. The navy's second reserve aerial mining squadron was established at Alameda in 1989, bringing the RH-53D and HM-19 to the bay area, and VA-304, the reserve's first A-6E squadron, transitioned from the A-7E in the same year. In addition to these squadrons, VR-55 and HS-85 operate from Alameda.

Also under the control of NAVAIRES Alameda are two Naval Air Reserve Centers (NARCEN), NARCEN Moffett Field, California, which has long been host to Naval Air Reserve programs, and NARCEN Barber's Point, Hawaii, the newest reserve force drilling site established in 1989. Moffett Field, the primary Maritime Patrol installation on the West Coast, is home to VP-91, Master Augment Unit 0180, and ten sustaining units.

NARTU Pt. Mugu, California

NAVAIRES Pt. Mugu—initially called NARTU Pt. Mugu—is located at the navy's Pacific Missile Test Center situated on the coast fifty miles northwest of Los Angeles. The airfield—next to the landmark Mugu Mt.—was

This illustration by noted aviation artist Wayne Percival shows a VFA-305 F/A-18 over the PMTC complex at Pt. Mugu.

constructed in the early days of WW II as a training base and a coastal defense installation. Reserve activity at Pt. Mugu was limited during the fifties and sixties, when testing sea- and air-launched missiles became its primary mission. The closure of southern California's major air reserve training complex at Los Alamitos in the late sixties prompted the move to Pt. Mugu, and the NARTU was commissioned in February 1971. Today, NARTU Pt. Mugu has been redesignated NAVAIRES Pt. Mugu and is home to VP-65, HCS-5, and VFA-305. NAVAIRES Pt. Mugu also administers training for over twenty sustaining units, and it exercises administrative control over the Naval Air Reserve Center, Lemoore, California. Reserve Carrier Air Wing Thirty's second F/A-18 squadron, VFA-303, is located at NAS Lemoore along with five sustaining units.

The NAVAIRES Pt. Mugu complex at the Pacific Missile Test Center.

NARTU Pt. Mugu was the first home of VP-65. "Papa Golf" Neptunes lined the ramp at the base in this early '70s photograph.

NARTU San Diego, California

Naval Air Station North Island, one of the navy's earliest aviation bases, hosted the arrival of a large reserve contingent in January 1970, when Naval Air Reserve Detachment North Island (NARDET) was established to support VP-63L3 and other units moving from Los Alamitos. Like Pt. Mugu, NAS North Island was destined to develop into a major reserve training activity as aviation programs relocated following transfer of the Los Alamitos base to the Air National Guard. In the summer of 1970 the NARDET was designated Naval Air Reserve Training Unit, North Island (NARTU) and then became Naval Air Reserve Unit (NARU) in December 1972. The command was redesignated NAVAIRES San Diego in April 1983.

Like other Naval Air Reserve commands, the mission of NAVAIRES San Diego is to administer training to selected reservists in aviation

One of the first West Coast air bases, NAS North Island has a rich heritage. Reservists trained at the base for many years before a formal command was established in the early '70s. This photo shows the current NAVAIRES training complex just behind the flag pole, with San Diego bay in the background.

What veteran—active or reserve—doesn't remember a parade and inspection in dress uniform? These San Diego reservists stand tall in "whites" for a command inspection in the early '80s.

programs with emphasis on readiness, recruiting, and retention. NAS North Island is also the location of Commander Naval Air Forces Pacific (COMNAVAIRPAC) Reserve Liaison Office, which provides a direct link between Commander Naval Air Reserve Force and the fleet type commander. The East Coast counterpart of the AirPac reserve liaison office is located at NAS Norfolk, Virginia.

One of the largest of the Naval Air Reserve Commands, NAVAIRES San Diego directs programs for six reserve force squadrons—two located at NAS North Island and four at NAS Miramar—and more than three dozen reinforcing and sustaining units. VR-57 and HSL-84 operate from the Coronado base. Naval Air Reserve Center Miramar is the location of VF-301 and VF-302, VAW-88, and VFC-13 and is also home to Commander, Carrier Air Wing Reserve, Thirty (CVWR-30). Over three thousand selected reserve and TAR (active-duty reserve specialists) personnel are assigned to components of the NAVAIRES San Diego command.

NARTU Whidbey Island, Washington

The closure of the naval air station at Sand Point, Washington, in 1969 marked the end of an era for reserve aviation in the Pacific Northwest. Situated close to Seattle, Sand Point traced its origins back to the earliest days of naval aviation when the first reserve units were formed following approval of Admiral Moffett's plan for a much-expanded corps. The base closure had little effect upon Naval Air Reserve squadrons and units because they were immediately relocated as a tenant at Naval Air Station, Whidbey Island, an active-duty base that had been requisitioned in the late thirties and commissioned in the summer of 1942. Whidbey Island, in the northern reach of Puget Sound, was easily accessible from the major population centers of Seattle and Tacoma, and the Sand Point units had little difficulty adapting to their new home.

Initially, NARTU Whidbey Island was home to two newly commissioned reserve squadrons, VP-69 and VS-83; a detachment of VR-51 operated C-118s as well. Today NARTU Whidbey is designated simply Naval Air Reserve Whidbey and is representative of other reserve "tenant" commands at major fleet bases where the Naval Air Reserve has made a large investment in facilities. Two relatively new reserve hangars provide space for VP-69's Orions and for the EA-6Bs of VAQ-309; a new transport hangar and air-terminal complex for VR-61 were dedicated in 1989, and in 1990, a new training and administration building replaced the WW II barracks that had been used by reservists since 1970.

The latest of the training and administration buildings built at active-duty bases is the Naval Air Reserve Whidbey Island complex. Dedicated in April 1990, it serves more than 1,300 selected reservists from the Pacific Northwest.

Table 8-1. Bases of the Naval Air Reserve: Summary

Activity	Date Comm.	Remarks
Akron	14 Jan 1948	Disestablished 1 Feb 1958
Anacostia	1926	Redesignated as NARTU 1945; moved to Andrews AFB 1962 and renamed NAF Washington
Atlanta	1940	Established as NRAB Chamblee; redesignated NAS 1943; relocated to Dobbins AFB 1959, and renamed NAS Marietta; renamed NAS Atlanta
Birmingham	15 Oct 1948	Redesignated as NARF 1956; disestablished 1 Oct 1957
Columbus	1 Apr 1946	Disestablished June 1959
Dallas	1941	Established as NRAB; redesignated NAS 1943
Denver	16 Feb 1947	Disestablished June 1959
Houston	1 Oct 1956	Established as Naval Air Reserve Facility (NARF); disestablished 1 Feb 1958
Great Lakes/Glenview	1923	Established as NRAB Great Lakes; moved to Glenview 1937; redesignated NAS Chicago/Glenview 1943; renamed NAS Glenview 1944
Grosse Ile/Detroit	1928	Established NRAB Grosse Ile; redesignated NAS 1945; relocated (Selfridge AFB) and redesignated NAF Detroit 1969
NARTU Jacksonville	1 Dec 1945	
NARTU Lakehurst	2 Jun 1947	Disestablished 1976
NAS Lincoln	15 Dec 1948	Disestablished 1 Feb 1958
NAS Livermore	1 Dec 1945	Disestablished late 1946
Long Beach/Los Alamitos	1928	Established as NRAB Long Beach; relocated & redesignated Los Alamitos 1942; disestablished 1976
Miami	—	Designated NARTU 1945; redesignated NAS Miami in 1951; redesignated NARTU, MCAS Miami in 1952; redesignated NARF in 1958; disestablished June 1959
Minneapolis	1927	Established as NRAB; redesignated NAS 1943; renamed NAS Twin Cities 1963; disestablished 1970
Memphis	1946	Redesignated NARTU 1959
New Orleans	1942	Relocated at Belle Chase-Callender Field 1958
New York	1923	Established as NRAB Ft. Hamilton; moved to Rockaway Beach; relocated to Valley Stream, 1929; moved to Floyd Bennett Field 1931; disestablished 1971
NAS Niagara Falls	18 Dec 1948	Disestablished June 1959
NARTU Norfolk	1946	
Oakland/Alameda	1928	Established as NRAB Oakland; moved to Livermore during WW II; relocated and redesignated as NAS Oakland 1946; moved to Alameda and redesignated NARTU 1961
NAS Olathe	1942	Redesignated NAS 1943; disestablished 1970
NARTU Pt. Mugu	1971	
NARTU San Diego	1 Dec 1945	Disestablished 1946; reestablished 1970; renamed NAVAIRES 1982
NARTU Santa Ana	1 Apr 1951	Disestablished June 1956
Seattle	1925	Established as NRAB Sand Point; redesignated NARTU 1945; redesignated NAS Seattle 1953; disestablished 1970
NAS Spokane	1 Sep 1948	Redesignated as NARF 1956; disestablished 1 Feb 1958
Squantum/South Weymouth	1923	Began as NRAB, redesignated NAS 1945, relocated and redesignated NAS South Weymouth 1953
NAS St. Louis	1925	Disestablished 31 Jan 1958
Philadelphia/Willow Grove	1929	Established as NRAB Philadelphia Navy Yard; relocated & redesignated NAS Willow Grove 1943
NARTU Whidbey Island	1969	Assumed reserve units from NAS Seattle

THE NEXT 75 YEARS

The first seventy-five years of the Naval Air Reserve saw the organization grow from one seaplane, flown and maintained by volunteer college students, to more than 450 state-of-the-art aircraft flown and maintained by the most experienced pilots in the navy. As the '80s gave way to the '90s, the Naval Air Reserve force enjoyed an excellent reputation and had performed superbly in every role it had been asked to fill. But regardless of how good a reserve force looks on paper, or how well reserve squadrons do during annual active duty for training, the true measure of a reserve force becomes apparent only under the ultimate challenge—an actual war. And just such a situation occurred in January 1991 when forces led by the United States commenced combat operations to liberate Kuwait.

The Naval Air Reserve has actually played an important role in the Middle East since August 1990 when Iraq invaded Kuwait. Many air reservists, particularly those assigned to sustaining/augmenting units, were activated and mobilized. Reservists assigned to medical and intelligence units were particularly in demand.

As Operation Desert Shield evolved into Operation Desert Storm, the Naval Air Reserve became even more involved. Detachments of hardware squadrons HCS-4, HCS-5, and HS-75, and VP-91 were activated as were the entire transport squadrons VR-55, VR-57, VR-58, and VR-59. More individuals with difficult-to-find skills were mobilized both from drilling units and the Individual Ready Reserve. By the end of January 1991, almost 2,300 naval air reservists had been recalled to active duty with more to come.

If the country or the politicians had any doubts about the value of a well-trained and ready reserve force, the events in the Middle East should have erased those doubts. Active-duty forces simply did not have available people with special skills and experience in sufficient numbers to meet the demands of so large-scale an operation as Desert Shield/Storm. With a trained and ready reserve, military planners could call up those units and individuals they needed to augment the active forces. From those forces not needed overseas, reservists filled in at home to plug gaps left by active-duty forces deployed abroad. In short, the system worked.

Operation Desert Shield/Storm was the vindication for those visionaries who believed that not only was a strong reserve force desirable but critical to our nation's defense. The many dollars and much effort expended since the 1970s to build a reserve force every bit as good as the regular navy paid big dividends in 1990. John Lehman, the chiefs of the Naval Air Reserve, and the thousands of reservists who built up the Naval Air Reserve from its nadir during the *Pueblo* mobilization can be proud as they see the results of their efforts at work in Saudi Arabia and Kuwait.

Unfortunately, memories can be short. Times change; threats come and go; politicians are elected and defeated. What does the future hold for the Naval Air Reserve?

No one has a crystal ball, of course, so any predictions about the future can be made only on the basis of an educated guess. But who is more qualified to give such an educated guess than the leaders of the past who have shaped and moulded our Naval Air Reserve force today? Listen to them, because they are the history of the Naval Air Reserve, and we all know that history repeats itself.

Rear Admiral Frederick Palmer

"To see where the Naval Air Reserve is going in the future, let's look at the past when reservists were called up and see how well they did in Korea. Before Korea, we had an extraordinary inversion of priorities. We had a small naval reserve force flying a lot and active-duty folks flying very little, if at all. At the same time, ships were being quickly decommissioned or mothballed.

"Remember, the time-frame from World War II to more combat in Korea was only five years. People had lots of memories. We also had the same equipment, ships and airplanes. It was immediately clear that there were not enough aircraft carriers or aircraft to sustain expected combat and operational losses. So, the reserves were mobilized.

"If you want the kind of reserve that can step right in and help, and I would certainly recommend it, then we need to take a close look now

"The first 75 years of the Naval Air Reserve have seen the organization grow from one seaplane, flown and maintained by volunteer college students, to more than 450 state-of-the-art aircraft flown and maintained by the best professionals in the navy."

as we see the regular navy receding in the number of aircraft, ships and people. This is no time to make a comparable cut in the Naval Air Reserve; in fact, we should increase the size of the reserve. The potential to react quickly to a situation that requires more people depends largely on a strong reserve across the board—army, air force, national guard and navy.

"If we find that the Cold War still has a few burning embers, we might need a force to be applied. Today, we're trying to balance the budget and eliminate the deficit. I hope we don't send a signal of weakness. We need to hold the line and continue beefing up the reserve with identical equipment that can be used quickly by well-trained personnel."

Former Secretary of the Navy John Lehman

"It is meet and just that the 75th anniversary year of the Naval Air Reserve is the year that we have won the cold war. The two events of course are not at all unrelated, the one being an important contributing cause of the other. Forty-five of those 75 years have been spent with Naval Air Reservists in the front line of every theater in every battle and in every showdown of the long cold war. But now all of that sacrifice, all of that valor, all of that professionalism has helped to end the cold war era. As the great alliance named for an ocean has watched in awe, its adversary alliance named for the land-locked capital of Poland has disintegrated. But now with the end of an era, the comfortable certitude that has formed the framework for our mission in the Naval Air Reserve is gone. We now are in an entirely new era, and while the Warsaw Pact is most certainly dead, its component forces are certainly not. The Russian armed forces are not diminished, nor are the Balkans visibly more stable outside the polarity of the cold war. While the threat of superpower war is much reduced, the next decade will probably see more violence and instability than any in the postwar period. The services must change fundamentally to cope with this less certain, more violent world. Most affected will be the army and the air force. Since 1942 they have been sized, equipped and trained for massive attrition warfare in Central Europe.

"Least affected will be the navy and marines. Whether we like it or not, we are a maritime nation. Our navy is the necessary manifestation of that reality. It existed before the Soviet Union and before the Communist Party, and it will remain, whatever form the evolution of the East Bloc may take. We have to be able—and be seen to be able—to ensure the security of the seas that link us to our allies, our commercial partners, our energy and our resources. We have to have the capacity to defeat any combination of adversaries seeking to interfere with our access to the seas. We must ensure that no enemy (including terrorists and drug lords) may use the seas as a medium of attack against us. And we must ensure that we have the use of the seas as a medium of applying force to terminate any conflict. As we mark the end of the first 75 years, we must reconfigure the Naval Air Reserve for the new post-cold-war era in which its mission will become even more important to the navy and the nation.

"As the immediate threat of Soviet aggression in the Persian Gulf, the Mediterranean, and the Pacific recedes dramatically (though perhaps only temporarily), the navy should adapt its operations accordingly. We still need at least 14 aircraft carriers. To preserve as much of the ready fleet as possible, the air reserve must be called upon to shoulder a larger

burden. The wartime tempo of our fleet operations should be significantly reduced. Instead of scrapping or mothballing carriers and squadrons, they should be shifted to the ready reserve and manned 50 percent by full-time active-duty personnel, and 50 percent by weekend warriors. They should be kept fully abreast of fleet upgrades and operate on weekends and for longer active-duty fleet exercises.

"For such a concept to work, the existing Naval Air Reserve structure must be modified and expanded, and navy personnel policies—focused entirely on career retention—must change accordingly. More pay, more assignment flexibility, more local recruiting for each home port, and more importance must be given to reservists.

"Officers and sailors on active duty, seeking to go into the active reserves, should not be treated as treasonous wimps. Many enlistees should be given the option of a two-year active-duty obligation followed by six years in the drilling reserves. Similarly, graduates of the Naval Academy, Naval Reserve Officer Training Corps and Officer Candidate School should be given the option of shorter active-duty obligations followed by longer drilling reserve obligations.

"The Naval Air Reserve in the 75 years of its history has proved that the professionalism unique to naval aviation can be maintained by citizen sailors when properly trained and motivated. Now more than

"History has shown time and time again that naval air reservists can be counted on to perform, and perform well, when their country needs them."

ever the nation needs to make use of this splendid elite force and the traditions and lessons that it embodies. The Naval Air Reserve should become the standard around which a new total force for the post-cold-war era is designed."

Rear Admiral Tommy F. Rinard, Former Commander Naval Air Reserve Force

"As we look to the future of the Naval Air Reserve and what we see today vis-à-vis the change in the Russian philosophies and strategies, I don't anticipate an extreme drawdown of the Naval Air Reserve. The force has to be maintained at least at its present level—if not increased—for obvious reasons. The economics of the Naval Air Reserve force become more important in a changing world where basically you are projecting a peacetime operation for an extended period.

"At the same time we must make sure that we have a balance between the Naval Air Reserve force and our active force. Too frequently, we forget there is a direct correlation between the size of the Naval Reserve and the size of our active forces. Since the reserve draws from the active forces for those veterans who have served at least one tour of active duty, then we must forecast also how many veterans are coming out of the active forces in order to come into the Naval Reserve. This applies to both surface and aviation forces. In these areas we must maintain a delicate balance in order not to overload the system and cause shortages in the Naval Air Reserve. Clearly, if you find yourself in a circumstance where you don't have proper manning, and you can't achieve proper manning because the people are not available from the active forces, then you have a reserve that cannot be mobilized, or if mobilized, cannot function properly because of a lack of personnel. This is a very sensitive area. The pilot training rate, for example, affects the Naval Air Reserve in the number and types of pilots who are available. So we have to remember that the Naval Air Reserve force and active-duty force, while separate activities, are still very much interdependent for our total defense effort.

"As we look to the future, what I would hope to see is a circumstance that would have the active force and reserve force viewed as one complete entity. As we procure new equipment for our active force, we must also provide identical equipment for the Naval Air Reserve in order to keep it totally current and readily available in the event of hostilities. As we drawdown active forces, it becomes imperative that the level of readiness in the Naval Air Reserve be totally maintained. This can only be done if we have properly trained personnel—both officer and enlisted—pilots, NFOs, and mechanics, and that they be equipped with state-of-the-art, identical equipment to that being utilized in the fleet.

"Over the years, I have been privileged to see a great change in this force. We have made giant strides in improving our product. The Naval Air Reserve force of the late '60s was, quite honestly, totally unusable, but not because of the people or their lack of dedication. Our naval reservists are some of the most dedicated people in our Navy. They give up weekends and vacations for the opportunity to participate in the navy and to provide their skills for the country. But before, we did not have them properly trained. We could not properly train them because we did not have squadrons that were self-sustaining. We did not have proper site support equipment to maintain the aircraft that were assigned, and of course, the aircraft were obsolete or at best obsolescent. Having worked ourselves out of this situation, we find now that we have achieved

164

The role of the Naval Air Reserve has never been more important than it is as we celebrate our 75th anniversary. The Naval Air Reserve of the future will become an even more vital part of our nation's defense. *(Photo by George Hall)*

a level of readiness that has cost a lot of dollars and a lot of time and effort on the parts of many people. This improved reserve force has been supported throughout the navy and by the navy secretariat. This is the type of support that is required if we are to maintain the Naval Air Reserve force at its current high state of readiness and its total mobilization capability. Clearly, today the force is able to mobilize immediately, and it can meet the threat of a combat situation anywhere in the world. I would see that to be the naval air reserve of the future. We have attained those capabilities, they have been achieved after long, arduous years working, training, rebuilding, and I would hope that we never let that level of capability wane, nor that we lose our dedication to having a properly structured, trained, and equipped force. It really can't work any other way."

Rear Admiral Richard K. Chambers, Commander, Naval Air Reserve Force

"The Naval Air Reserve has been and always will be a critical component of our nation's defense. Its ability to augment active forces in times of emergency has been the difference between success and failure, between freedom and occupation, in conflicts ranging from World War I to the Iraqi invasion of Kuwait.

"Mobilization readiness will always be a major role of the Naval Air Reserve, but it is no longer the only role our reservists play. Now more than ever, the reservist is working alongside his active-duty counterpart on a daily basis rather than 'waiting in the wings' for a national emergency. This trend has evolved over recent years, and will continue to accelerate in the future for several reasons. First of all, the Naval Air Reserve has finally been given the funding and equipment to truly integrate with and contribute to the active-duty navy. The second consideration is economic. Since reservists perform many of the tasks typically assigned to active-duty forces, but at a much lower cost, it makes sense to transfer some of the active-duty load to reserve components. Additionally, the navy retains expensively trained, highly experienced people who bring unique expertise to their warfare specialty. Increased use of the Naval Air Reserve saves defense dollars without compromising operational readiness, a bargain in anybody's book.

"The changing politics of the '90s are another strong argument for the Naval Air Reserve. Glasnost, disarmament treaties and the relaxation of world tensions have brought calls for cutbacks in the active forces and military budget. While every citizen hopes and prays for a long-standing peace, we would be foolish to ignore the harsh lessons of history and fall into a condition of military unpreparedness. We must always be able to respond to aggression by the Saddam Husseins of this world, even if we are unable to support the large standing force we have maintained in recent years. In this contradictory environment, a strong Naval Air Reserve is essential. With a trained, experienced and ready reserve, we can reduce our standing forces, work for peace and save money without compromising our ability to respond to unexpected hostilities.

"Clearly, the role of the Naval Air Reserve has never been more important than it is as we celebrate our 75th anniversary. The Naval Air Reserve of the future will become an even more vital part of our nation's defense. As a result, reservists will be asked to give more than ever. While this may involve personal sacrifices, history has shown time and time again that naval air reservists can be counted on to perform, and perform well, when their country needs them. F. Trubee Davison, David Ingalls, Jack Shea, George Bush and thousands of other Naval Air Reservists have built the Naval Air Reserve on a tradition of excellence, patriotism and dedication. I have no doubt that present and future naval air reserve citizens will carry on this proud tradition of service to their country. Trained, experienced, dedicated and ready: this will be the Naval Air Reserve of the next 75 years."

APPENDICES

A. LEADERS OF THE NAVAL AIR RESERVE—1945–1990

CNARESTRA

Former Chiefs of Naval Air Reserve Training 1945–1970

Rear Admiral
F. D. Wagner
Nov 45 to Dec 45

Rear Admiral
E. C. Ewen
Dec 45 to Feb 48

Rear Admiral
R. F. Whitehead
Feb 48 to July 49

Rear Admiral
A. K. Doyle
July 49 to Aug 51

Rear Admiral
L. A. Moebus
Aug 51 to Nov 52

Rear Admiral
D. V. Gallery
Nov 52 to Nov 56

Rear Admiral
H. H. Caldwell
Nov 56 to Oct 58

Rear Admiral
A. Smith, Jr.
Oct 58 to May 60

Rear Admiral
A. W. McKechnie
May 60 to Oct 61

Rear Admiral
W. I. Martin
Oct 61 to May 63

Captain
E. M. Stever
May 63 to July 63

Rear Admiral
G. P. Koch
July 63 to Sep 65

Rear Admiral
R. L. Fowler
Sep 65 to Jan 67

Rear Admiral
W. S. Guest
Mar 67 to Dec 69

Rear Admiral
H. E. Greer
Dec 69 to Apr 72

COMNAVRESFOR

Former Commanders of the Naval Reserve Force established 1973

Rear Admiral
J. D. Ramage
CNARESTRA May 72–Feb 73
Feb 73–Apr 73

Vice Admiral
D. W. Cooper
Apr 73–May 74

Vice Admiral
P. N. Charbonnet
Aug 74–Sep 78

Rear Admiral
F. F. Palmer
Oct 78–Sep 83

Vice Admiral
R. F. Dunn
Oct 82–Dec 83

Vice Admiral
C. J. Kempf
Dec 83–May 87

COMNAVAIRESFOR

Former Commander of the Naval Air Reserve Force established 1983

Rear Admiral
T. F. Rinard
Oct 83–Sep 87

B. MAJOR COMMANDS OF THE NAVAL AIR RESERVE

Naval Air Stations, Naval Air Facilities, Naval Air Reserves, and Units Attached, Including Co-located Wings and Squadrons*

NAVAL AIR FACILITY WASHINGTON, D.C.

VAQ-209
VP-68
VR-48
COMFLELOGSUPPWING DET
   WASH., D.C.

NR NAVAIRSTCM 2366
NR NAVAIRSYS 0166
NR NISRO 0166
NR CTF 168 0566
NR NAVOPINTCN 0666
NR NORA WASH 0966
NR DNI ESSUPU 0166
NR NAVSPASUR 0266
NR VP-1166
NR VP-1649
NR CARGRU 0466
NR NAVOPINTCN 0566
NR NIAC 0166
DEF ATTACHE 0166
NR NAVAIRSYS 0466
NR ASWOC 466

NR NORA WASH 0166
NR FOSIC ERP 0166
NR FAIRKEF 1066
NR DIAHQ 0266
NR NAIRSYS 0366
NR NAIRSYS 0266
NR NADOC 0166
NR CNO INTEST 0166
NR NIC 0166
NTIC 1566
NR CNO INTPL 0166
NR NAS KEF 1066
NTIC 1466
NR NISCOM 0166
NR NAVSPCOM 0166
NR ABFC FMP MMF H

NR NAVAIRSYS 1366
NR CTF 168 HQ 0466
NR ACNO OP05 0166
NR NICSEC 0166
NR ASWOC 966
NR CV-62 0166
NR CVN-69 0166
NR VR-24 COMP 366
NR CNO PLANS 0166
NR DIA CURINT 0166
NR NH PAX RVR 0166
NR WASH M/D 0166
NR OSD TECTRS 0166
NR GVTU 6666
NR ASCVTU 0666
NR IVTU 0106

NAS ATLANTA, GA

VA-205
VR-46
NR NVMDCL KYWT0267
NR COMPHIBGRU2 867
NR NORA ATL 1567
NR CARGRU 0667
NR FIRSTEURLNT 867
NR FIRSTEURLNT 967
NR NAS JAX 0167

NR NAS CECFLD 0667
NR NISRO 1407
NTIC 0709
NTIC 1209
NR NTSC 0167
NR VA-2267
NR NS ROTA 0167
NR CNAVEUR INT 167
NR CV-59 0167

NR NAVAIRSYS 1367
NR 4 MAWMDMG41 DTB
NR CV-60 0167
NR VR-24 467
NR NAS ATL M/D 0167
NR GVTU 6767
NR IVTU 0108

*Listing effective as of 31 January 1991.

NAVAL AIR STATION DALLAS, TX

COMFLELOGSUPPWING
VF-201

VF-202
VR-59
NR NAVPRO DLS 0470
NR NAVOPINTCN 0770
NR CV-66 0270
NR VF-1170
NR NORA DAL 1570
NR CARGRU 0170
NR FIRST PAC 370
NR FIRST PAC 470
NR NAVAIRSYS 0570
NR NAS NI DET 170
NR NAS MIRAMAR 170

NR COMFAIRWP 0170
NR US CINCSO 0111
NR DIAHQ 0670
NR NAS KWEST 170
NR TRAWG 2 D 170
NR TRAWG 3 D 270
NR TRAWG 4 D 370
NR NWEF 0170
NR NICHQ 0170
NR NICHQ DET 0170
NR VR-24 COMP 270
NR 4MAW MEDMAG 41
NR CARGRU 770

NR FIRST PAC 1070
NR NAVAIRSYS 0770
NR NAS M/D 0170
NR NAS MED 0170
NR US CINCSO 0270
NR GVTU 7070
NR ASCVTU 0970
NR IVTU 0111
NR CV-67 DET 170
NR COM 7FLT 111

Naval Air Reserve Center Denver, CO

NR NAVAIRSYCM 1471
NR NAVOPINCEN 1071
NAS MIRAMAR 0171
NR FIRST PAC 1371

NR FIRST PAC 571
NR NAS FALLON 0271
NR NAF ATSUGI 0171
NR NSIU 0171

NR IPAC 0171
NR CV-61 0171
NR CV-41 0171
NR NH WHIDBEY 0371

NR GVTU 7170
NR IVTU 0118

NAS GLENVIEW, ILL

VP-60
VP-90
VR-51
NR NAVOPINTCN 0872
NR VP-0622
NR VP-0172
NR NAC 0172
NR NORA GLNVW 0272
NR NORA GLNVW 1672
PATWING 472

NR NAVALANT D 172
NR FRSTERLANT 1472
NR FRSTERLANT 1572
NR NAVAIRSYS 0672
NR NS ADAK 0172
NR NS MIDWAY 0972
NR NISRO 1972
NTIC 1313
NR NAS ANGUM 0772
NR DEFINTERROG 0372

NR NAS 0172
NR VR COMPONENT 872
NR 4MAWMDMACG 43
NR CVN-69 0272
NR NAS GLVWM/D0172
NR ABFC FMP MMF F
NR GVTU 7272
NR ASCVTU 0872
NR IVTU 0113

Naval Air Reserve Center Minneapolis, MN

NR DIAHQ 0878
NR CVN-70 0278
NR CVN-71 0178
NR FIRST PAC 178

NR FIRSTPAC 278
NR NAS PTMUGU 0178
NR NAS KEF 0378
NR NIAC 0278

NR DEFINTEROG 0118
NR 4MAW MDMSG 47
NR CV-63 0178
NR GVTU 7872

NR ASCVTU 1078
NR IVTU 0116

NAVAL AIR FACILITY (NAF) DETROIT, MI

VP-93
VR-62
NR CVN-69 0373
NR CV-66 AMRCA 0473
NR ASWOC 273
NR NORA DET 1773
NR FRSTERLANT 1673

NR FRSTERLANT 1773
NR DEF DCMENT 0102
NTIC 0305
NR NAF SIG 0573
NR NAF LAJES 0473
NR DIAHQ 0705
NR VR-24 573

NR NH PAX RVR 0373
NR BRDCL 0173
NR ABFC FMP MMF E
NR GVTU 7373
NR IVTU 0114

Naval Air Reserve Center Columbus, OH

NR NAVOPINTCN 0909
NR FRSTERLANT 1081
NTIC 0605
NTIC 0581

NR NAS OCEANA 0181
NTIC 1005
NR CVN-70 DET 0281
NR CVN-65 0181

NR NH PAX RVR 0281
NR GVTU 8173
NR IVTU 0114

NAVAL AIR RESERVE JACKSONVILLE, FL

VP-62
VR-58
HS-75
CVWR 20 (CECIL)
VFA-203 (CECIL)
NR CVWR-20 0174
NR CTF 168 0208
NR VFA-2074
NR NAS CECFLD 0174
NR CV-59 FRSTL 0174
NR NAS JAX 0274
NR 4MAWMED MAG42/A
NR CINCSOINT 0108

NAS MAYPORT 0174
NR VFA-1074
NR HS-1197
NR HS-1535
NR VP-0545
NR DIAHQ 0408
NR ASWOC 374
NR ASWOC 574
NR NORA JAX 1274
PATWING 1174
NR HELO ASWG 174
NR FIRSTEURLNT 774
NR NADEP 0474

NR NISRO 1274
NTIC 1108
NR MEDCL NOLA 0174
NR ABFC FMP MMF A
NR VP-2474
NR VS-0174 (CECIL)
NR USCINCLANT 0108
NR BRDCL 0174
NR GVTU 7474
NR ASCVTU 0774
NR IVTU 0208

NAVAL AIR RESERVE POINT MUGU, CA

VFA-305
HCS-5
VP-65
NR NAVPRO BRBK 0670
NR PATWING 1076
NR CV-41 0276
NR CVN-65 0376
NR VP-0476

NR LEMOORE DT 3476
NR VFA-1476
NR NORA PT MUGU 2276
NR NWC CHINA LK 276
NR NAVAIRSYS 1076
NR NAF CHILAKE 176
NR FLTACT OKI 0176
NR NAS CUBI PT 176

NR NAVAIRSYS 1376
NR CV-62 INDY 0176
NR VP-0919
NR NH LEMOORE 0276
NR GVTU 7676
NR ASCVTU 0276

Naval Air Reserve Center Lemoore, CA

VFA-303
NR LAT WINGPAC 190
NR NAS LEMORE 3490

NR NH LEMOORE 0190
NR GVTU 9076

NAVAL AIR RESERVE MEMPHIS, TN

VR-60
VP-67
NR NAVPRO ST LOUIS
NR NORA MPHIS 1179
NR CV-60 0279
NR USCINCLANT 0209

NR NAS CUBI PT 0179
NR CVN-72 0179
NR DFDOCUMENT 0218
NR FRSTERLANT 1379
NR NISRO 1779
NR NAF MIS 0779

NR NIC 0218
NR BRDCL 0179
NR NAS MED 0179
NR ABFC FMP MMF G
VR GVTU 7979
NR IVTU 0123

Naval Air Reserve Center Olathe, KS

NR CV-41 MDWAY 0183
NR NAS MOFFETT FLD 883
NR CVN-70 VNSN 0183

NR NH WHIDBEY 0283
NR GVTU 8379

NAS NEW ORLEANS, LA

VR-54
VFA-204
VP-94
COMFLELOGSUPPWING DET
NR CV-60 0382
NR BRCL NPTC 0182
NR VR COMP 0282
NR DIAHQ 0910
NR NAVSTA ROTA 0182
NR VP-5682
NR NORA NO 1482

NR FAIR MED 1082
NR FRSTERLANT 1182
NR FRSTERLANT 1282
NR NADEP 0582
NR NISRO 2210
NR NISRO 2310
NR NISRO 2182
NR NISRO 2010
NR NAS NOLA 3682
NR VA-2082
NR ASWOC 682

NR CARGRU 0282
NR TRAWG 1 D 182
NR TRAWG 5 D 282
NR TRAWG 6 D 382
NR VR-24 COMP 182
NR 4MAW MED HQ BR
NR 4MAW MDMG 46DTB
NR GVTU 8282
NR IVTU 0109
NR CV-63 DET 0482

NAVAL AIR RESERVE NORFOLK, VA

VAW-78
VR-56
HCS-4
VFC-12 (OCEANA)
HM-18
COMRESPATWINGLANT
NR NAVAIREAST 0286
NR CVN-72 ABLN 0186
NR VAW-1086
NR TACGRU 2 286
NR TACRON 24
NR VC-686 (OCEANA)
NR LANTJIC 0186
NR FIRSTEU LAN 486

NR NMITC 0186
NR NORA NFLK 2186
NR FOSIF ROTA 186
NR FOSICNRV RU186
NR NAVAIRLANT 1086
NR TACRON 23
NR DIAHQ 0307
NR NADEP 0386
NR NISRO 0986
NTIC 0406
NR NAS NORVA 2186
NR SLANT INTL 0186
NR VRC 4086
NR RESPATWNGLT 186

NR LNTFLTIMAGU 186
NR NAVSTA BRCL 106
NR CLANT INTEL 186
NR 4MAW MDMG 46DTA
NR NMC NORFOLK 0186
NR NALNTOPNTL 0186
NR LTFLTPOAVU 0286
NR VF-1486 (OCEANA)
NR VA-0686 (OCEANA)
NR NAS MED/DEN 0186
NR GVTU 8686
NR IVTU 0206

NAVAL AIR RESERVE ALAMEDA, CA

VA-304
VR-55
HM-19
HS-85
NR COM 3FLT 0187
NR CTF 168 0620
NR STK WARCTR 0287
NR VA-1287
NR HS-128
NR NORA ALM 1887

NR AIRPAC SUP 0187
NR FIRST PAC 1187
NR FIRST PAC 1287
NR NAVAIRSYS 1187
NR NADEP 0187
NTIC 0920
NTIC 0820
NR NAS ALAMEDA 187
NR NISRO 2687
NR NAVOPINTCN 0320

NR CVN-65 0187
NR INTCENPAC 0220
NR 4 MAW MDMG 42
NR CARGRU 0387
NR NAS M/D 0187
NR GVTU 8787
NR ASCVTU 0187
NR IVTU 0120

Naval Air Reserve Center Barbers Pt., HI

NR ABFC FMP MMF D
NR CVN-68 NMTZ 0268
NR FOSICPAC 0168
NR ASWOC 1168
NR FOSIFWPAC 0168

NR NAS BRS PT 0168
NR IPAC 0468
NR GVTU 6887
NR IVTU 0119

Naval Air Reserve Center Moffett Field, CA

VP-91
COMRESPATWING PAC
NR NAS NORIS 0180
NR ABFC MMF DET D

NR ASWOC 1080
NR RESPATWING 0180
NR ASWOC 880
NR NAVAIRSYS 1380

NR VP MAU MFLD 0180
NR ABFC FMP MMF C
NR NAS MFT M/D 0280
NR NAS MFT MED 0180

NR NAS MFT DEN 0180
NR GVTU 8087

NAVAL AIR RESERVE WHIDBEY ISLAND, WA

VAQ-309
VR-61
VP-69
NRINTCENPAC 0522
NR NAVAIRSYCM 1589
NR ADAK DET 0189
NR CV-62 0389
NR VP-1789
NR MATWING 289
NR ASWOC 0389
NR NORA WHID IS 2089

NR FIRSTPAC 1689
NR NISRO 2422
NR NAS WHID 4089
NR DIAHQ 0522
NR FIRSTPAC 1489
NR CARGRU 0589
NR CVN-68 0289
NR VA-0689
NR NH/DC WHID 0189
NR GVTU 8989
NR IVTU 0189

NAVAL AIR STATION SOUTH WEYMOUTH, MA

VP-92
HSL-74
NR NAVPRO STFD 0291
NR NAVPRO LYNN 0391
NR NIAC 0391
NR CV-67 JFK 0291
NR ASWOC 191
NR NORA SO WEY 109
NR FIRSTEURLNT 191
NR FIRSTEURLNT 291
NR NAVAIRSYS 0891

NR NS ROTA 0391
NR NISRO 0301
NTIC 0202
NR NAS BRUNS 4291
NR NISRO 0201
NR NAS SO WEY 1291
NR ASWOC 791
NR NAVAIRSYS 1391
NR CV-67 0191
NR VR COMPONENT 691
NR 4MAWMDMG 49DTA

NR VP MAU 0191
   (BRUNSWICK)
NR NAS MED/DEN0191
NR NAVMED 0191
NR GVTU 9191
NR ASCVTU 0591
NR IVTU 0101
NTIC 0102
NR NISRO 0502
NR NAVOPINTCN 0101

NAVAL AIR STATION WILLOW GROVE, PA

VP-64
VP-66
VR-52
HSL-94
NR NAVAIRSYCM 0993
NR NAS LAJES 0193
NR NORA WG 1193
NR CTF 168 0102
NR CVN-71 0193
NR MDZ INTEL 0102
NR SIGONELLA 0193
NR NAVOPINTCN 0102
NR LNTFLTIMAGU 193
NR NORA WILGVE 109
NR PAT WING 593
NR NAVAIRLNT D 293
NR FIRSTEURLNT 593
NR FIRSTEURLNT 693
NR FIRSTEURLNT 393
NR DIAHQ 193
NR NADC WRMN 0293

NR NATC PAX 0193
NR NADC WRMN 0193
NR MED/DEN 0193
NR NISRO 0893
NTIC 0102
NR NAS BERDA 0693
NR NISRO 0602
NR NAS WILGRV 1993
NR NAS KEF 0293
NR NAVOPINTCN 0402
CMSRF 6TH FLT 193
NR CV-66 0193
NR NAS 0193
NR VR COMPONENT 793
NR 4MAW MEDMAG 49
NR BRDCL 0193
NR GVTU 9393
NR ASCVTU 0493
NR IVTU 0102
NR DETOPS 0102

Naval Air Reserve Antisubmarine Warfare Training Center

NAVAL AIR RESERVE SAN DIEGO, CA

VR-57	NR FIRST PAC 794	NR VS-0294
HSL-84	NR FIRST PAC 894	NR NAP OPINT 0194
COMHELWINGRES	NR NAVAIRSYS 1294	NR TACRON 1194
NR CTF 168 0794	NR NADEP 0294	NR TACRON 1294
NR FITCPAC 0194	NR NISRO 2819	NR 4MAW MDMG 46
NR HS-246	NR NISRO 2794	NR CV-61 0194
NR ASWWING PAC 194	NR NAS NORIS 194	NR NAS NI MED 0194
NR NORA SDIEGO 199	NR INTEL CPAC 0319	NR NAS NI DEN 0194
NR AIRPAC SUP 0294	NR COMTACGR 1 0194	NR GVTU 9494
NR NAVAIRPAC 1094	NR SURFPAC 0994	NR ASCVTU 1194
NR DEFINTERROG 0219	NR CMCAMGRUPAC 194	NR IVTU 0121
NR FIRST PAC 919	NR ASWOC 1294	NR CVN-72 DET 0194

Naval Air Reserve Center Miramar, CA

VF-301	CVWR-30	NR PACFLTIMAGU 185	NR VAW-0285
VF-302	NR VF-1285	NR F/A WING PAC 185	NR MCAS MD/DN 0815
VAW-88	NR VC-885	NR VF-1485	NR GVTU 8594

COMMANDER CARRIER AIR WING RESERVE 20

VF-201
VF-202
VFA-203
VFA-204
VA-205
VAW-78
VAQ-209

COMMANDER CARRIER AIR WING RESERVE 30

VF-301
VF-302
VFA-303
VFA-305
VA-304
VAW-88
VAQ-309

COMMANDER RESERVE PATROL WING PACIFIC

VP-60
VP-65
VP-67
VP-69
VP-90
VP-91

COMMANDER RESERVE PATROL WING ATLANTIC

VP-62
VP-64
VP-66
VP-68
VP-92
VP-93
VP-94

COMMANDER HELICOPTER WING RESERVE

HS-75
HS-85
HM-18
HM-19
HCS-4
HCS-5
HSL-74
HSL-84
HSL-94

COMMANDER FLEET LOGISTIC SUPPORT WING

VR-46
VR-48
VR-51
VR-52
VR-54
VR-55
VR-56
VR-57
VR-58
VR-59

VR-60
VR-61
VR-62
VFC-12
VFC-13
FLEET LOGISTICS SUPPORT
   WING DET NEW ORLEANS
FLEET LOGISTICS SUPPORT
   WING DET WASHINGTON
   D.C.

C. SQUADRONS OF THE NAVAL AIR RESERVE

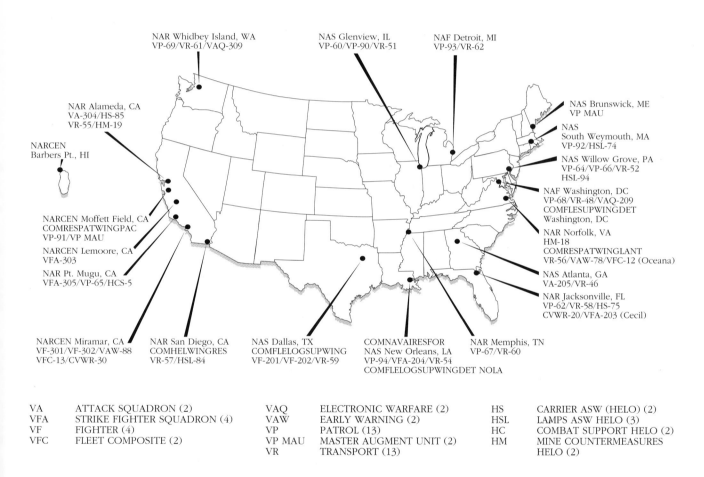

NAR Whidbey Island, WA
VP-69/VR-61/VAQ-309

NAS Glenview, IL
VP-60/VP-90/VR-51

NAF Detroit, MI
VP-93/VR-62

NAR Alameda, CA
VA-304/HS-85
VR-55/HM-19

NARCEN
Barbers Pt., HI

NARCEN Moffett Field, CA
COMRESPATWINGPAC
VP-91/VP MAU

NARCEN Lemoore, CA
VFA-303

NAR Pt. Mugu, CA
VFA-305/VP-65/HCS-5

NAS Brunswick, ME
VP MAU

NAS
South Weymouth, MA
VP-92/HSL-74

NAS Willow Grove, PA
VP-64/VP-66/VR-52
HSL-94

NAF Washington, DC
VP-68/VR-48/VAQ-209
COMFLESUPWINGDET
Washington, DC

NAR Norfolk, VA
HM-18
COMRESPATWINGLANT
VR-56/VAW-78/VFC-12 (Oceana)

NAS Atlanta, GA
VA-205/VR-46

NAR Jacksonville, FL
VP-62/VR-58/HS-75
CVWR-20/VFA-203 (Cecil)

NARCEN Miramar, CA
VF-301/VF-302/VAW-88
VFC-13/CVWR-30

NAR San Diego, CA
COMHELWINGRES
VR-57/HSL-84

NAS Dallas, TX
COMFLELOGSUPWING
VF-201/VF-202/VR-59

COMNAVAIRESFOR
NAS New Orleans, LA
VP-94/VFA-204/VR-54
COMFLELOGSUPWINGDET NOLA

NAR Memphis, TN
VP-67/VR-60

VA	ATTACK SQUADRON (2)	VAQ	ELECTRONIC WARFARE (2)	HS	CARRIER ASW (HELO) (2)
VFA	STRIKE FIGHTER SQUADRON (4)	VAW	EARLY WARNING (2)	HSL	LAMPS ASW HELO (3)
VF	FIGHTER (4)	VP	PATROL (13)	HC	COMBAT SUPPORT HELO (2)
VFC	FLEET COMPOSITE (2)	VP MAU	MASTER AUGMENT UNIT (2)	HM	MINE COUNTERMEASURES
		VR	TRANSPORT (13)		HELO (2)

AIR RESERVE SQUADRONS

VF-201 "Hunters" NAS Dallas,
TX
Aircraft: 12 F-14A; tail letters:
AF-100
CVWR-20
Established 25 July 1970

VF-202 "Superheats" NAS Dallas,
TX
Aircraft: 12 F-14A; tail letters:
AF-200
CVWR-20
Established 25 July 1970

An F-14A pilot from VF-201 logs an arrested landing aboard USS *Dwight D. Eisenhower*. (Photo by George Hall)

F-14 Tomcats from VF-201 and VF-202 at NAS Dallas await the start of the day's operations. (Photo by George Hall)

An F-14A of VF-202 flies over the *Eisenhower* (CVN-69) during a CVWR-20 cruise aboard the nuclear carrier in 1989. (Photo by George Hall)

VF-301 "Infernos" NAS Miramar,
  CA
Aircraft: 12 F-14A; tail letters:
  ND-100
CVWR-30
Established 1 October 1970

VF-302 "Stallions" NAS Miramar,
  CA
Aircraft: 12 F-14A; tail letters:
  ND-200
CVWR-30
Established 21 May 1971

An F-14 from VF-301 flies over southern California.

An F-14A from VF-302 maneuvers in the vertical off the coast of California. The Tomcat's variable-sweep wings give the fighter excellent slow speed characteristics with the wings positioned full forward, as above, while enabling supersonic speeds with the wings swept full back.

VA-205 "Green Falcons" NAS
   Atlanta, GA
Aircraft: 10 A-6E, 4 KA-6D; tail
   letters: AF-500
CVWR-20
Established 1970

VA-304 "Firebirds" NAS
   Alameda, CA
Aircraft: 10 A-6E, 4 KA-6D; tail
   letters: ND-400
CVWR-30
Established July 1970

A KA-6D assigned to VA-205, NAS Atlanta. The "Green Falcons" transitioned to the A-6E Intruder from the A-7E Corsair in 1990, giving CVWR-20 a medium-attack capability for the first time.

An A-6E from VA-304 during carrier qualifications. VA-304 was the first reserve squadron to receive a medium-attack aircraft when they transitioned from the A-7E. (Photo by George Hall)

VFA-203 "Blue Dolphins" NAS
   Cecil Field, FL
Aircraft: 12 F/A-18A; tail letters:
   AF-300
CVWR-20
Established July 1970

VFA-204 "River Rattlers" NAS
   New Orleans, LA
Aircraft: 12 F/A-18A; tail letters:
   AF-400
CVWR-20
Established July 1970

VA-203 became the first East Coast Reserve Squadron to transition from the A-7E to the F/A-18A. The squadron, originally established at NAS Jacksonville, FL, has flown A-4Ls, A-7As, and A-7Es. Upon acceptance of its first F/A-18 in October 1989, the squadron changed its designation to VFA.

A VFA-204 F/A-18 from NAS New Orleans. This squadron transitioned from A-7Es in the spring of 1991.

VFA-303 "Golden Hawks" NAS
  Lemoore, CA
Aircraft: 12 F/A-18A; tail letters:
  ND-300
CVWR-30
Established July 1970

VFA-305 "Lobos" NAS Pt. Mugu,
  CA
Aircraft: 12 F/A-18A; tail letters:
  ND-500
CVWR-30
Established July 1970

F/A-18s from VFA-303. The versatile Hornet can be reconfigured on short notice for either the fighter or attack mission. (Photo by George Hall)

VFA-305 was established as Attack Squadron 305 at NAS Los Alamitos, CA. The squadron moved to Pt. Mugu, CA, in 1970 when Los Alamitos was closed. They transitioned from the A-4L to the A-7A and A-7B, which they flew until receiving their first Hornet in 1987. The "Lobos" were the first reserve squadron to participate in a "RED FLAG" exercise at Nellis AFB. (Photo by George Hall)

VAW-78 "Fighting Escargots"
  NAS Norfolk, VA
Aircraft: E-2C; tail letters:
  AF-600–604
CVWR-20
Established July 1970

VAW-88 "Cotton Pickers" NAS
  Miramar, CA
Aircraft: E-2C; tail letters:
  ND-600–604
CVWR-30
Established July 1970

An E-2C from VAW-78 prepares to depart NAS Norfolk on a training flight. VAW-78 flew the E-1 and E-2B before receiving its current, state-of-the-art Hawkeye.

An E-2C Hawkeye from VAW-88 searches for targets from its vantage point high in the sky. Effective early-warning detection capability is critical to the defense of the aircraft carriers, and the E-2C is the best carrier-based early-warning aircraft the Navy has. (Photo by George Hall)

VAQ-209 "Star Warriors" NAF
Washington, D.C.
Aircraft: EA-6B; tail letters:
AF-604–608
CAW-20
Established October 1977

VAQ-309 "Axe Men" NAS
Whidbey Island, WA
Aircraft: EA-6B; tail letters:
ND-604–608
CAW-30
Established December 1979

VAQ-209 transitioned to the EA-6B in the summer of 1990. This photo shows one of the squadron's first aircraft undergoing acceptance checks prior to its first flight.

An EA-6B crew from VAQ-309 prepares for carrier qualifications. VAQ-309 transitioned to the Prowler from the EA-6A, a much less capable two-seat version of the Intruder adapted to the electronic-warfare mission.

HS-75 "Emerald Knights" NAS
Jacksonville, FL
Aircraft: SH-3H; tail letters:
NW-610–616 (AF when
mobilized)
COMHELWINGRES
Established July 1970

HS-85 "Golden Gaters": NAS
Alameda, CA
Aircraft: SH-3H; tail letters:
NW-610–615 (ND when
mobilized)
COMHELWINGRES
Established July 1970

The venerable SH-3 Sea King still serves in the fleet as well as in the Naval Air Reserve. This aircraft from HS-75 provides plane guard duties in addition to its primary mission of antisubmarine warfare.

HCS-4 "Red Wolves" NAS
Norfolk, VA
Aircraft: HH-60H; tail letters:
NW-200–208
COMHELWINGRES
Established October 1989

HCS-5 "Firehawks" NAS
Pt. Mugu, CA
Aircraft: HH-60H; tail letters:
NW-300–308
COMHELWINGRES
Established October 1988

With the receipt of this new HH-60H Seahawk, HAL-4 retired its HH-1K gunships and assumed a new identity as HCS-4. The "Red Wolves" were the Navy's only helicopter gunship squadron when they were established in 1976, and they performed the mission with distinction for thirteen years. (Photo by George Hall)

This HH-60H Seahawk is flown by HCS-5. HCS-5 was the first squadron in the Naval Air Reserve to receive the HH-60H.

HM-18 "Norsemen" NAS
Norfolk, VA
Aircraft: RH-53D; tail letters:
NW-610–616
COMHELWINGRES
Established October 1986

HM-19 "Golden Bears" NAS
Alameda, CA
Aircraft: RH-53D; tail letters:
NW-620–625
COMHELWINGRES
Established January 1989

Pilots from HM-18 prepare to start the engines of their RH-53D. HM-18 was the first "minesweeping" squadron to enter the Naval Air Reserve.

An RH-53D from HM-19 returns to NAS Alameda after a training flight. The establishment of a second airborne mine-counter-measures squadron gave the Naval Air Reserve a minesweeping capability on both coasts.

HSL-74 "Demon Elves" NAS
South Weymouth, MA
Aircraft: SH-2G; tail letters:
NW-40–47
COMHELWINGRES
Established January 1985

HSL-84 "Thunderbolts" NAS
North Island, CA
Aircraft: SH-2G; tail letters:
NW-00–07
COMHELWINGRES
Established March 1984

Three SH-2s of HSL-74 NAS South Weymouth fly over Boston Harbor. The helicopters display two different marking schemes, reflecting the Navy's changing policy.

HSL-84 became the Naval Air Reserve's first LAMPS squadron when it transitioned from the SH-3 in 1984.

HSL-94 "Titans" NAS Willow
Grove, PA
Aircraft: SH-2G; tail letters:
NW-20–27
COMHELWINGRES
Established October 1985

HSL-94 was established in 1985, giving the Naval Air Reserve a total of three LAMPS squadrons.

VR-46 "Peach Tree" NAS Atlanta, GA
Aircraft: C-9B; tail letters: JS
Established March 1981

Reserve squadrons fly airlift missions around the world virtually every day of the year. This C-9B is from VR-58. (Photo by George Hall)

VR-48 (no call sign) NAF Washington, DC
Aircraft: C-20; tail letters: JR
Established October 1980

VR-51 "Flamin' Hookers" NAS Glenview, IL
Aircraft: C-9B; tail letters: RV
Established November 1970

VR-52 "Taskmasters" NAS Willow Grove, PA
Aircraft: C-9B; tail letters: JT
Established June 1972

Arguably the most productive and visible of all Naval Air Reserve communities, the VR transport squadrons, equipped with the C-9/DC-9 aircraft, have proved their worth time and time again. In combat operations in Grenada and Lebanon, the Naval Air Reserve C-9s brought out the wounded and brought in supplies and material. During the military buildup in Saudi Arabia as part of Operation Desert Shield, reserve VR squadrons once again played a critical role in moving the massive numbers of people and quantity of material required by the threat. This C-9 is flown by VR-51.

VFC-12 "Omars" NAS Oceana,
    VA
Aircraft: 7 A-4F, 5 TA-4J; tail
    letters: JY-00–14
FLSW
Established September 1973

VFC-13 "Saints" NAS Miramar,
    CA
Aircraft: 7 A-4F, 5 TA-4J; tail
    letters: UX-00–14
FLSW
Established September 1973

A VFC-12 A-4F and a new F-14A(plus) from VF-101 return from
an ACM training mission. (Photo by Peter Mersky)

This A-4F "Super Fox" from VFC-13 is carrying a specially cali-
brated pod on its centerline that is used to track aircraft during
air-combat-maneuvering training flights. With these pods on the
participating aircraft, flights conducted in the instrumented training range (designated TACTS) can be fully documented and re-
played on a large video screen following the flight. (Photo by
George Hall)

VR-54 "Revelers" NAS New
    Orleans
Aircraft: C-130T; tail letters: CW
Established June 1991

VR-55 "Minutemen" NAS
    Alameda, CA
Aircraft: C-9B; tail letters: RU
Established April 1976

VR-56 "Globemasters" NAS
    Norfolk, VA
Aircraft: C-9B; tail letters: JU
Established July 1976

VR-57 "Conquistadors" NAS
    North Island, CA
Aircraft: C-9B; tail letters: RX
Established April 1978

VR-58 "Sun Seekers" NAS
Jacksonville, FL
Aircraft: C-9B; tail letters: JV
Established November 1977

VR-59 "Lonestar Express" NAS
Dallas, TX
Aircraft: C-9B; tail letters: RY
Established November 1982

VR-60 "Volunteer Express" NAS
Memphis, TN
Aircraft: C-9B; tail letters: RT
Established October 1982

VR-61 "Islanders" NAS Whidbey
Island, WA
Aircraft: C-9B; tail letters: RS
Established October 1982

VR-62 "Motowners" NAF Detroit,
MI
Aircraft: C-9B; tail letters: JW
Established July 1985

A C-9B from VR-57 on the ramp.

COMRESPATWINGLANT

VP-62 "Broad Arrows" NAS
Jacksonville, FL
P-3C Update III; tail letters: LT
Established November 1970

VP-64 "Condors" NAS Willow
Grove, PA
Aircraft: P-3B TACNAVMOD; tail
letters: LU
Established November 1970

VP-66 "Liberty Bells" NAS
Willow Grove, PA
Aircraft: P-3B TACNAVMOD; tail
letters: LV
Established November 1970

VP-68 "Blackhawks" NAF
Washington, DC
Aircraft: P-3B TACNAVMOD; tail
letters: LW
Established November 1970

VP-92 "Minutemen" NAS South
Weymouth, MA
Aircraft: P-3B TACNAVMOD; tail
letters: LY
Established November 1970

The seven Maritime Patrol Squadrons assigned to Reserve Patrol Wing Atlantic pose for this group photo during a change-of-command ceremony. From top to bottom the squadrons are: VP-68, VP-94, VP-93, VP-92, VP-66, VP-64, and VP-62.

VP-93 "Executioners" NAF
Detroit, MI
Aircraft: P-3B TACNAVMOD; tail
letters: LH
Established July 1976

VP-94 "Crawfishers" NAS New
Orleans, LA
Aircraft: P-3B TACNAVMOD; tail
letters: LZ
Established November 1970

COMRESPATWINGPAC

VP-60 "Cobras" NAS Glenview, IL
Aircraft: P-3B TACNAVMOD; tail letters: LS
Established November 1970

VP-65 "Tridents" NAS Pt. Mugu, CA
Aircraft: P-3B TACNAVMOD; tail letters: PG
Established November 1970

VP-67 "Golden Hawks" NAS Memphis, TN
Aircraft: P-3B TACNAVMOD; tail letters: PL
Established November 1970

VP-69 "Totems" NAS Whidbey Island, WA
Aircraft: P-3B TACNAVMOD; tail letters: PJ
Established November 1970

VP-90 "Lions" NAS Glenview, IL
Aircraft: P-3B TACNAVMOD; tail letters: LX
Established November 1970

VP-91 "Stingers" NAS Moffett Field, CA
Aircraft: P-3C Update III; tail letters: PM
Established November 1970

The P-3 squadrons assigned to Reserve Patrol Wing Pacific, from right to left: VP-60, VP-65, VP-67, VP-69, VP-90, and VP-91.

THE NAVAL INSTITUTE PRESS

WINGS AT THE READY
75 Years of the Naval Air Reserve

Designed by Pamela L. Schnitter

Set in Garamond Light and Futura Extra Bold
by Waldman Graphics, Inc.
Pennsauken, New Jersey

Printed on 60-lb. Glatco Matte
by The John D. Lucas Printing Company
Baltimore, Maryland

Bound in Holliston Roxite B Linen
by American Trade Bindery
Baltimore, Maryland

TED WILBUR
ASAA